Edexcel

higher

GCSE Modular Mathematics

unit 1

Keith Pledger

Gareth Cole

Peter Jolly

Graham Newman

Joe Petran

www.heinemann.co.uk

✓ Free online support
✓ Useful weblinks
✓ 24 hour online ordering

01865 888058

Heinemann

Inspiring generations

Heinemann is an imprint of Pearson Education Limited,
a company incorporated in England and Wales, having
its registered office at Edinburgh Gate, Harlow, Essex, CM20 2JE.
Registered company number: 872828

Heinneman is a registered trademark of Pearson Education Limited

© Harcourt Education Ltd, 2006

First published 2006

10 09 08
10 9 8 7 6 5 4 3 2 1

British Library Cataloguing in Publication Data is available from the British Library
on request.

ISBN: 978 0 435585 30 3

Typeset by Tech-Set Ltd, Gateshead, Tyne and Wear
Original illustrations © Harcourt Education Limited, 2006
Cover design by mccdesign
Printed in China (CTPS/01)
Cover photo: Digital Vision©

Acknowledgements
This high quality material is endorsed by Edexcel and has been through a rigorous quality
assurance programme to ensure that it is a suitable companion to the specification for both
learners and teachers. This does not mean that its contents will be used verbatim when
setting examinations nor is it to be read as being the official specification – a copy of which
is available at www.edexcel.org.uk.

The publisher's and authors' thanks are due to Edexcel Limited for permission to reproduce
questions from past examination papers. These are marked with an [E]. The answers have
been provided by the authors and are not the responsibility of Edexcel Limited.

The authors and publisher would like to thank the following individuals and organisations
for permission to reproduce photographs: Photos.com pp**1**, **7**, **29**, **50**, **63**; Corbis pp**3**,
4, **10**, **14** top, **43**, **78**; MorgueFile/Cahilus p**5**, Empics pp**6**, **75** bottom; Getty Images/
PhotoDisc pp**11**, **14** bottom, **16**, **34**, **40**, **64**, **65**, **69**, **82**, **85**; Jane Hance p**18**; iStockPhoto
pp**68**, **75** top; Pearson Education Ltd/Jules Selmes p**72**; MorgueFile/Motorshots p**83**

Every effort has been made to contact copyright holders of material reproduced in this
book. Any omissions will be rectified in subsequent printings if notice is given to the
publishers.

Publishing team

Editorial	Katherine Pate, James Orr, Evan Curnow, Lindsey Besley, Lyn Imeson, Jim Newall, Elizabeth Bowden
Design	Christopher Howson
Production	Helen McCreath
Picture research	Chrissie Martin

Websites
There are links to relevant websites in this book. In order to ensure that the links are
up-to-date, that the links work, and that the sites aren't inadvertently linked to sites that
could be considered offensive, we have made the links available on the Heinemann website
at www.heinemann.co.uk/hotlinks. When you access the site, the express code is **3843P**.

Tel: 01865 888058 www.heinemann.co.uk

Quick reference to chapters

Contents

4 Relationships and trends in data

5 Probability

6 More probability

About this book

This book has been carefully matched to the new two-tier modular specification for Edexcel GCSE Maths. It covers everything you need to know to achieve success in Unit 1. The author team is made up of the Chief Examiner, the Chair of Examiners, Principal Examiners and Senior Moderators, all experienced teachers with an excellent understanding of the Edexcel specification.

Key features

Chapters are divided into **sections**. In each section you will find:
- **key points**, highlighted throughout like this

  - A **histogram** is used to display continuous grouped data.

- **examples** that show you how to tackle questions
- an **exercise** to help develop your understanding.

Each chapter ends with a **mixed exercise** and a **summary of key points**. Mixed exercises, which include past exam questions marked with an [E], are designed to test your understanding across the chapter.

Hint boxes are used to make explanations clearer. They may also remind you of previously learned facts or tell you where in the book to find more information.

A census is usually only practical for small populations.

An **examination practice paper** is included to help you prepare for the exam at the end of the unit.

Answers are provided at the back of the book to use as your teacher directs.

Quick reference and detailed Contents pages

Use the thumb spots on the **Quick reference page** to turn to the right chapter quickly.

Use the detailed **Contents** to help you find a section on a particular topic. The summary and reference codes on the right show your teacher the part(s) of the specification covered by each section of the book. (For example, HD3b refers to Handling data, section 3 Collecting data, subsection b.)

Teaching and learning software

References to the *Heinemann* Edexcel GCSE Mathematics **Teaching and learning software** are included for you and your teacher. (The number refers to the relevant chapter from the linear course on which the software is based.)

5 Data collection sheets

1 Collecting data

1.1 Tally charts, questionnaires and two-way tables

5 Data collection sheets

- You can collect and display data in a **tally chart**.
- Data you collect is called **primary data**. Data that has been collected by other people is called **secondary data**.

Example 1

Zamia collects fossils. Here is a list of the number of fossils she collected on each of 30 days.

8	4	7	1	5	2
5	2	5	4	6	12
11	5	6	6	6	4
1	6	9	3	11	3
5	4	6	7	10	8

Design a data capture sheet on which this data can be collected. Record the data on your data capture sheet.

A **data capture sheet** is any kind of chart or table you use to collect data.

The numbers of fossils are discrete data.
A suitable data capture sheet is a tally chart.

Discrete data can be counted.

Number of fossils	Tally	Frequency
1–3	卌		6
4–6	卌 卌 卌	15
7–9	卌	5
10–12	||||| 4

Remember to use 卌 to represent 5.

The smallest data value is 1. The largest is 12. Grouping the numbers of fossils in threes makes the data easier to manage.

Example 2

A set of 30 times in seconds is recorded, but the last result is missing.

12.8	10.0	4.3	16.1	5.6	18.2	14.3	11.6	22.0	18.3
22.1	5.9	13.5	3.2	11.5	10.7	15.3	4.2	7.8	8.8
6.5	17.0	7.4	12.9	13.2	11.7	23.0	16.4	15.3	

Continuous data is measured. These times are continuous data.

Record this data in the frequency table below.

Time (t) seconds	Tally	Frequency
$0 < t \leqslant 5$		
$5 < t \leqslant 10$		
$10 < t \leqslant 15$		
$15 < t \leqslant 20$		
$20 < t \leqslant 25$		

What could be done about the missing result?

> The class intervals must not overlap or have gaps between them.

Time (t) seconds	Tally	Frequency
$0 < t \leqslant 5$	|||	3
$5 < t \leqslant 10$	⧕ ||	7
$10 < t \leqslant 15$	⧕ ||||	9
$15 < t \leqslant 20$	⧕ ||	7
$20 < t \leqslant 25$	|||	3

If 30 results are needed then you need to record one more result. But if you do not *have* to have 30 results for the survey, just use the 29 results.

- When you are writing questions for a **questionnaire**
  - be clear what you want to find out and what data you need
  - ask short, simple questions
  - provide tick boxes with possible answers
  - avoid questions which are too vague, too personal, or which may influence the answer.

> **5** Identifying good questions

> Personal or 'leading' questions may be a source of bias. They may prevent people answering truthfully.

Example 3

Jon is collecting data on the types of sport people watch on TV. In his questionnaire he asks the question

　　'You like watching sport on TV, don't you?'

(a) Explain why the above question is a poor one.
(b) Write two good questions Jon could ask.

(a) The question is a poor one because it is leading. It actually tells people, or at least suggests to them that they *do* like watching sport on TV.

(b) The first question should be something like

1 Do you enjoy watching sport on TV? Yes No (Delete as appropriate)

If you answered 'Yes', please answer question 2.

2 Tick three boxes to show your three favourite sports to watch on TV.

Snooker ☐   Horse racing ☐

Rugby ☐   Cricket ☐

Tennis ☐   Other ☐

Football ☐

If you ticked 'Other', please specify ....

• You can use a **two-way table** to record data grouped into categories.

Example 4

This two-way table shows information on the types of holiday that 100 people chose.
Complete the table.

	Beach	Lakes and mountains	Cities	Totals
Men	28		10	53
Women		16	15	
Totals				100

The number of Lakes and mountains holidays chosen by men must be

53 (the total number of men) − (28 + 10) = 53 − 38 = 15

The total number of women must be

100 (the total number of people) − 53 (the number of men) = 100 − 53 = 47

The total number of Beach holidays chosen by women is

47 (the total number of women) − (16 + 15) = 47 − 31 = 16

This information now gives the following.
The total for Beach holidays is 28 + 16 = 44
The total for Lakes and mountains is 15 + 16 = 31
The total for Cities is 10 + 15 = 25

So the completed table is

	Beach	Lakes and mountains	Cities	Totals
Men	28	**15**	10	53
Women	**16**	16	15	**47**
Totals	**44**	**31**	**25**	100

Exercise 1A

1 George and Asif are carrying out a survey on the food students eat in the college canteen. George writes the question

'Which foods do you eat?'

Asif says this question is too vague.

Write down three ways in which the question could be improved.

2 A student wanted to find out how many pizzas adults ate. He used this question on a questionnaire.

'How many pizzas have you eaten?'

☐   ☐

A few   A lot

(a) Write down **two** things that are wrong with this question.

(b) Design a better question that the student can use to find out how many pizzas adults eat.
You should include some response boxes.   [E]

3 Thirty-two people order drinks in a cafe one evening. Here is a list of the drinks they order.

Coffee	Cola	Lemon	Tea	Coffee	Coffee	Tea	Coffee
Tea	Lemon	Coffee	Cola	Tea	Orange	Tea	Lemon
Cola	Cola	Coffee	Orange	Cola	Coffee	Lemon	Cola
Coffee	Tea	Orange	Cola	Milk	Coffee	Coffee	Tea

Design and complete a tally chart and frequency table for this information.

4 Jenny and Reyhana are collecting information about how people will vote in the General Election.
Design a suitable data capture sheet they could use.

5 Karen conducts a survey into how long people can hold their breath under water. She has the following list of 60 times in seconds (to the nearest second).

```
32 41 27 16 22 23 13  8 11 28 37 54 64 12 70
44 18 19 22 30 15 43 17 21 27 34 35 36 42 19
73 65 28 17 16 45 51 27 14 43 12 36 11  9 10
55 67 18 23 24 16 10 43 44 52 56 18 17 26 58
```

Design and complete a grouped frequency table which records these times in five-second intervals. Start with the class interval
     $0 < \text{time} \leqslant 5$

6 A group of 80 students were asked about the number of videos and
   DVDs they owned. Some of the results are provided in this two-way
   table.

	Videos	DVDs	Totals
Boys	21		38
Girls		27	
Totals			80

   Copy and complete the two-way table.

7 A reporter recorded the gender and age of the 35 people at a
   meeting of the European Parliament in Strasbourg.
   Here are her results.

Male 33	Female 24	Female 58	Male 29	Male 48
Male 45	Female 57	Male 44	Male 46	Female 40
Female 49	Male 52	Female 33	Female 37	Female 52
Male 42	Male 54	Male 48	Male 56	Male 52
Male 49	Male 59	Male 56	Female 37	Female 34
Male 49	Male 39	Male 48	Male 49	Male 55
Female 32	Female 29	Male 37	Female 32	Male 50

A session of the European
Parliament is held in Strasbourg
each month.

   Copy this data capture sheet and record the data on it.

Age (years)	Male	Female	Total
21–30			
31–40			
41–50			
51–60			
	Total	Total	35

8 For each of the investigations below, suggest how you could
   collect the data. Is the data primary or secondary data?
   (a) Investigating prices of flat screen TVs
   (b) Investigating whether 15–18-year-olds eat five portions of
       fruit/vegetables each day
   (c) Investigating SATs results for a local primary school
   (d) Investigating residents' views on traffic in their street
   (e) Investigating the numbers of road accidents per year in Britain.

1.2 Taking a sample

- The **population** is the complete set of items under consideration.

- A **census** collects information from every member of a population.

- A **sample** collects information from only part of a population.
  The larger the sample, the more reliable the results.

- A **biased sample** is not representative of the whole population.

A census is usually only
practical for small
populations.

The **National Census**
collects information for
every household in the UK.
The information is collected
every ten years. The next
Census will be in 2011.

Example 5

Brenda wants to find out what people think about Radio 1.
She considers asking three different groups of people:

Group A: People in her class
Group B: People listening to Radio 1
Group C: The people at a school fete

Which group of people should she ask?

Group C •————————— This group is likely to be a mix of ages.

5 Bias

Group A are all the same age group and unlikely to be representative of people in general. Group B all like Radio 1, so are not representative of the whole population.

Example 6

A company produces baked beans in tins. It wants to check the quality of the baked beans in the tins.
Give one reason why the company should **not** take a census of the tins.

A census collects information from every member of a population. This means that all the tins would be opened! A sample of the tins would be better.

The size of the sample is important. A large sample would be too expensive; a small sample may not give an accurate picture.

Exercise 1B

For each question select the most appropriate group of people to ask, A, B or C.

	Data needed	Who to ask
1	What people think about chess	A: The people in a shopping centre B: The people in a youth group C: Chess players
2	What people think about Mexican food	A: Mexican people B: People in a supermarket C: Men in a football club
3	If people in the neighbourhood are in favour of the Night Club	A: People at the local cinema B: Cleaners at the Night Club C: People in the Night Club

4 A factory is about to open a new staff restaurant.

(a) Give a reason why the restaurant manager should conduct a census survey to find out what the restaurant should offer on its menu.

(b) What is the population for this survey?

5 Tina wants to find out about the average age of female hockey players in the UK.

Give one reason why she should not take a census of female hockey players in the UK.

1.3 Sampling methods

5 Sampling

- In a **random sample** every member of the population has an equal chance of being chosen.

Example 7

As part of her handling data coursework, Sally wishes to take a random sample of 30 used cars so that she can record their ages and values. To do this she is going to use the advertisements in *Car Trader* magazine. The magazine has 200 pages and there are 40 advertisements on each page.

Describe two ways in which Sally could take a random sample of size 30.

Method 1

She could cut out all of the advertisements, screw them up and put them in a bag, shake the bag and pick out 30 advertisements.

Method 2

She could number each page in the magazine from 1 to 200, and number each advertisement on each page from 1 to 40. She could then use her calculator to generate a random number between 0 and 1. Multiplying this random number by 200 and rounding it to the nearest integer identifies a page in the magazine.

A second random number between 0 and 1, multiplied by 40 and rounded to the nearest integer identifies the advertisement on the page. She could do this 30 times to take her sample.

If the process chooses the same advertisement more than once, she should ignore this result and generate random numbers to select another.

> Advertisements are printed on both sides of a page, so she would need two copies of the magazine.

> Make sure you know how to generate random numbers on your calculator.

- In a **selective** (or **systematic**) **sample**, every nth item is chosen.

Example 8

A company called Kayman's produce drinks in cans. They wish to take a selective sample of 5% of a large batch of cans of orange drink. The cans are filled by machine and then travel to the packing area on a conveyor belt.

Explain how Kayman's could take this selective sample.

5% means 1 in every 20, so they need to check every 20th item. To find the first item to check, they should generate a random number between 0 and 1.

Multiplying this by 20 and rounding to the nearest integer gives a random number between 1 and 20.

Suppose the random number is 8. Kayman's should then sample the 8th, 28th, 48th, … can that passes on the conveyor belt, and so on.

- In a **stratified sample** the population is divided into groups (called strata) and each group is randomly sampled.

Example 9

James is examining the factors which influence the value of used cars.

He has recorded data for three makes of car: **Ford**, **Toyota** and **Mercedes**.

He has also categorised the cars according to engine size: **under 1600 cc** or **1600 cc and over**. His results are:

	Ford	Toyota	Mercedes	Total
Under 1600 cc	72	31	18	121
1600 cc and over	41	11	27	79
Total	113	42	45	200

James wishes to take a stratified sample of 40 cars from this data. This sample must be fairly representative.

How many Mercedes with an engine of 1600 cc or above should James include in his sample?

In his total population, James has 200 cars.
Of these, 27 are Mercedes with engine size 1600 cc and over.

As a proportion of the total, this is $\frac{27}{100} = 0.135$.

James's total sample is to be 40. So, to be fairly representative, the number of Mercedes 1600 cc and over included in the sample should be $\frac{27}{200} \times 40 = 5.4$. Round down to 5 cars, since it must be a whole number.

Another method is:
40 is one-fifth of 200.
One-fifth of 27 = 27 ÷ 5 = 5.4

Exercise 1C

1   As part of a survey, Kelly needs to interview some patients in a hospital. There are 1200 patients on the hospital register.
    (a) Explain how Kelly could select a random sample of 30 patients to interview.
    (b) Explain how Kelly could take a selective sample of 4% of the patients.

2   Tony is investigating the factors which influence the price of second-hand caravans. He has categorised the caravans by the number of berths as:
    2-berth   4-berth   6-berth
    and as:
    Touring   Static

Here are his results.

	2-berth	4-berth	6-berth
Touring	92	166	34
Static	16	26	66
Totals	108	192	100

Tony wishes to take a stratified sample of 50 caravans.

(a) How many of the caravans in his sample should be static 6-berth caravans?

(b) How many of the caravans in his sample should be 2-berth touring caravans?

3 (a) Explain the differences between a random sample, a selective sample and a stratified sample.

(b) Give an example of when it might be best to use
  (i) a stratified sample
  (ii) a random sample
  (iii) a selective sample.

4 Jennifer is investigating house prices. She is using the advertisements from *Property* magazine. The magazine has 250 pages with 50 advertisements on each page.
Jennifer requires a random sample of 80 advertisements.
Describe how she could take such a sample.

5 There are 1400 students at Maple School. They are distributed across the year groups and by gender as in the table below.

	Girls	Boys
Year 7	180	170
Year 8	164	160
Year 9	137	142
Year 10	128	118
Year 11	100	101

The governors of the school are considering a possible alteration to the school day. Before any decision is made the Chair of Governors decides to seek the views of the students by interviewing 60 of them.
She wishes to take a stratified sample of 60 students which will be representative across the year groups and the gender divide.

(a) How many boys in Year 10 should the Chair of Governors interview?

(b) Work out the total number of Key Stage 3 students she should interview.

6   Explain how market research company could take a 2% selective
    sample of people whose names appear in the local telephone
    directory.

Activity – Collecting continuous data

(Go to www.heinemann.co.uk/hotlinks, and insert the express code
3843P and click on this activity.)

Use the Mayfield database to select a random sample of 50 male
students from Key Stage 4 (KS4).

Design a two-way table to record the height and weight for each
student. You should have five categories horizontally and five
categories vertically.

Comment on your results.

Mixed exercise 1

1   Hattie wants to carry out a survey on the number of hours people
    listen to the radio. She writes the question

    'Do you listen to the radio?'

    never ☐   sometimes ☐   often ☐   always ☐

    (a) Give one reason why this is not a good question.
    (b) Write a suitable question she could use.

2   The table gives information about the attendance at a basketball
    match.

	Male	Female	Total
18 and under	21		
19–25			32
26 and over	10	7	
Total	54		100

    (a) Copy and complete the table.
    (b) What percentage of the people were
         (i) 18 and under   (ii) 19–25-year-old females?

3   Bob asked 100 adults which one type of music they enjoyed.
    They could choose Jazz or Rock or Classical or Folk music.
    The two-way table shows some information about their answers.

	Jazz	Rock	Classical	Folk	Total
Men	12		19	4	52
Women		23			
Total	21			11	100

Copy and complete the two-way table.

4 Petros wants to find out how teenagers communicate with each other.

He designs a questionnaire.

Here are two of his questions.

The questions are **not** suitable.

For each question, write down a reason why.

(a) Do you prefer to communicate with your best friend by mobile or by email?

Yes ☐   No ☐

(b) How many email addresses do you have?

1 ☐   2 ☐   3 ☐   4 ☐   [E]

5 Daniel is conducting a survey into the amount of money that teenagers spend on magazines.

He uses this question on a questionnaire.

'How much money do you spend on magazines?'

£1 ☐   £2 ☐   £3 ☐

Write down **two** things that are wrong with this question.   [E]

6 Explain how to take a selective sample of 10% of the 800 students in a school.

7 Rani is carrying out a survey on social events for a tennis club. The choices are disco, barbecue and garden party. She wants to analyse her results according to the ages of the club members.

Design a suitable data capture sheet she could use to collect the information.

8 You are conducting a survey into the lengths of words used in two magazines.

(a) Describe how you could take a random sample of 20 words from each magazine.

(b) How could you improve the reliability of your sample?

9 Mrs Agadino, the manager of a restaurant, wishes to select a random sample of 30 of her employees.

(a) Explain how she could do this.

(b) Write down one advantage, and one disadvantage, of increasing the size of her sample.

10 The table shows information about the age distribution of male students at an FE college.

Age (years)	Number of male students
16	97
17	224
18	179

Kate is carrying out a survey into students' part-time jobs. She uses a stratified sample of 60 male students according to age.

(a) Calculate the number of students of each age for her sample of 60.

Kate also uses a stratified sample of 60 female students according to age.
In the college there are 193 female students aged 17 years.
In Kate's sample there are 22 female students aged 17 years.

(b) Calculate the smallest possible number of female students there could be in the college.

Summary of key points

1 You can collect and display data in a **tally chart**.

2 Data you collect is called **primary data**. Data that has been collected by other people is called **secondary data**.

3 When you are writing questions for a **questionnaire**
  - be clear what you want to find out and what data you need
  - ask short, simple questions
  - provide tick boxes with possible answers
  - avoid questions which are too vague, too personal, or which may influence the answer.

4 You can use a **two-way table** to record data grouped into categories.

5 The **population** is the complete set of items under consideration.

6 A **census** collects information from every member of a population.

7 A **sample** collects information from only part of a population. The larger the sample, the more reliable the results.

8 A **biased sample** is not representative of the whole population.

9 In a **random sample** every member of the population has an equal chance of being chosen.

10 In a **stratified sample** the population is divided into groups (called strata) and each group is randomly sampled.

11 In a **selective** (or **systematic**) **sample**, every nth item is chosen.

2 Representing and processing data

2.1 Pie charts and stem and leaf diagrams

- A **pie chart** shows how data is shared or divided into different categories.

Example 1

The table gives information about car theft in four countries.

Country	Number of cars stolen (thousands)
UK	340
Japan	310
Italy	246
France	304
Total	1200

Draw a pie chart for this information.

On the pie chart, the angle for the UK is

$$\frac{340}{1200} \times 360° = 102°$$

$\frac{340}{1200} = \frac{\text{number for UK}}{\text{total}}$
There are 360° in a full circle.

The other angles are

Japan: $\frac{310}{1200} \times 360° = 93°$

Italy: $\frac{246}{1200} \times 360° = 73.8° = 74°$ (to the nearest degree)

France: $\frac{304}{1200} \times 360° = 91.2° = 91°$ (to the nearest degree)

Check: 102 + 93 + 74 + 91 = 360 ✓

You cannot draw 0.2° accurately.

So the pie chart is

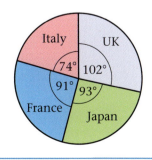

Use a protractor to draw the angles.

Example 2

The pie chart gives information about religious beliefs in the USA.

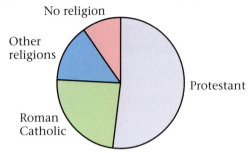

No religion

Other religions

Protestant

Roman Catholic

Work out the percentage that each sector in the pie chart represents.

The angle for Protestant is 187°.

So the percentage shown by the Protestant sector is
$\frac{187}{360} \times 100 = 51.94\%$ or 52% (to 2 s.f.)

The percentages shown by the other sectors are

Roman Catholic: $\frac{86}{360} \times 100 = 23.88\%$ or 24%

Other religions: $\frac{51}{360} \times 100 = 14.16\%$ or 14%

No religion: $\frac{36}{360} \times 100 = 10\%$

> Measure the angles with a protractor.

- A **stem and leaf diagram** shows the shape of a distribution and keeps all the data values. It needs a **key** to show how the stem and leaf are combined.

> **10** Drawing stem and leaf diagrams

Example 3

The heights in cm of 30 gym users are recorded below.

170	167	172	185	159	176	186	179	168	201
164	191	182	183	169	177	173	186	183	192
149	181	171	169	173	184	188	173	179	168

Represent this data as a stem and leaf diagram.

```
14 | 9
15 | 9
16 | 4, 7, 8, 8, 9, 9
17 | 0, 1, 2, 3, 3, 3, 6, 7, 9, 9
18 | 1, 2, 3, 3, 4, 5, 6, 6, 8
19 | 1, 2
20 | 1
```

Key: 20|1 means 201 cm

> Use the first two digits as the 'stem'.

> Write the 'leaves' in ascending order.

Exercise 2A

1 The table gives information about religious beliefs in the UK.

Christian	71.6%
Muslim	2.7%
Hindu	1%
Other religions	1.6%
No religion	23.1%

Draw a pie chart to represent this information.

2 The pie chart gives information about PC ownership in four countries.

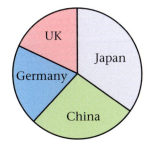

The total number of PCs in these four countries is 198 million. Work out the number of PCs in each country.

3 The costs, in £, of single rooms in 24 hotels are listed below.

110	118	125	110	134	132	169	125
127	141	110	111	120	149	99	159
120	125	127	180	163	170	109	115

Represent this information as a stem and leaf diagram.

4 Thirty people took part in a sponsored run. The amounts, in £, that they raised were:

77	68	43	117	98	91	68	51	81	102
43	57	69	60	72	101	92	113	49	58
84	82	75	48	53	62	81	70	68	64

Represent this information as a stem and leaf diagram.

2.2 Histograms with equal class intervals

- A **histogram** is used to display continuous grouped data.
- A **frequency polygon** shows the general pattern of data represented by a histogram.
- In a histogram the **area** of each rectangular bar represents the frequency for that class interval.

Example 4

A dentist recorded the time, in minutes, to treat each of 52 patients.
Her results are summarised in the frequency table.

Time t (minutes)	Frequency
$0 \leqslant t < 5$	8
$5 \leqslant t < 10$	6
$10 \leqslant t < 15$	17
$15 \leqslant t < 20$	10
$20 \leqslant t < 25$	7
$25 \leqslant t < 30$	4

(a) Draw a histogram for this information.

(b) Draw a frequency polygon on your histogram.

(a) The histogram is

For histograms with
equal class intervals,
plot the frequency
on the vertical axis.
Section 2.3 shows
you how to draw
histograms with
unequal class
intervals.

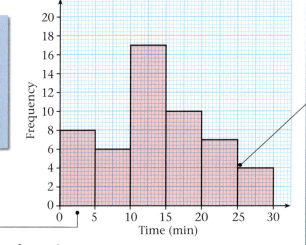

There are no gaps between
the bars, because time is a
continuous variable.

The class
intervals are
equal widths.

(b) The frequency polygon is

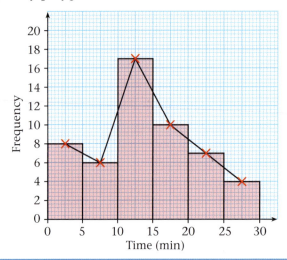

To draw the frequency
polygon, mark the mid-
points of the bars and
join them with straight
lines.

If you are asked to draw
a frequency polygon, you
do not need to draw the
histogram first. Join the
mid-points of the class
intervals.

Example 5

The frequency polygons show the times, in seconds, for 50 boys and 50 girls to hold their breath.

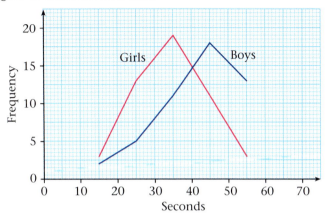

Frequency polyg... can be drawn on t... same axes to compar... distributions.

Comment on the ability of these boys and girls to hold their breath.

In general the boys can hold their breath for longer.

More of the boys have times further to the right along the time axis.

Exercise 2B

1 Harriet measured the temperature, in °C, of 60 drinks from a vending machine.

Here are her results.

59	78	81	63	65	67	75	61	82	48	49	67
64	57	73	41	60	42	52	73	78	68	70	75
65	74	62	67	86	78	60	64	59	78	86	56
58	87	73	54	77	67	52	89	71	47	76	72
72	80	55	88	70	43	60	74	68	79	75	68

(a) Copy and complete the grouped frequency table.

Temperature, t (°C)	Tally	Frequency
$40 \leqslant t < 50$		
$50 \leqslant t < 60$		
$60 \leqslant t < 70$		
$70 \leqslant t < 80$		
$80 \leqslant t < 90$		

(b) Draw a histogram to represent this information.

˄ speed camera records the speeds of 100 vehicles on a motorway. The results are shown in the table below.

Speed, s (mph)	Frequency
20 < s ⩽ 30	8
30 < s ⩽ 40	12
40 < s ⩽ 50	19
50 < s ⩽ 60	22
60 < s ⩽ 70	30
70 < s ⩽ 80	6
80 < s ⩽ 90	3

(a) Draw a histogram for this information.

(b) Draw a frequency polygon on your histogram.

3 The table provides some information about the mass, in grams, of 60 letters.

Mass, m (g)	Frequency
20 < m ⩽ 30	8
30 < m ⩽ 40	12
40 < m ⩽ 50	16
50 < m ⩽ 60	14
60 < m ⩽ 70	10

Represent this information on a frequency polygon.

4 The frequency polygons show the ages, in years, of the trees in two woods.

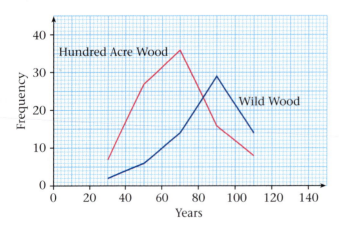

(a) Comment on the age of the trees in each wood.

(b) Comment on the number of trees in each wood.

2.3 Histograms with unequal class intervals

- In a histogram with unequal class intervals, the vertical axis shows **frequency density**.
- **Frequency density** $= \dfrac{\text{frequency}}{\text{class width}}$

  or

  Frequency density $= \dfrac{\text{frequency}}{\text{class width in standard class intervals}}$

Example 6

The frequency table gives information on ages of people in a yoga class.

Age, a (years)	Frequency
$0 < a \leqslant 20$	12
$20 < a \leqslant 30$	15
$30 < a \leqslant 35$	15
$35 < a \leqslant 40$	20
$40 < a \leqslant 50$	10
$50 < a \leqslant 60$	12
$60 < a \leqslant 90$	9

The class intervals are not equal.

Draw a histogram for this information

(a) using the class widths given

(b) using a standard class interval of 5 years.

(a)

Age, a (years)	Class width (years)	Frequency	Frequency density
$0 < a \leqslant 20$	20	12	$\frac{12}{20} = 0.6$
$20 < a \leqslant 30$	10	15	$\frac{15}{10} = 1.5$
$30 < a \leqslant 35$	5	15	$\frac{15}{5} = 3$
$35 < a \leqslant 40$	5	20	$\frac{20}{5} = 4$
$40 < a \leqslant 50$	10	10	$\frac{10}{10} = 1$
$50 < a \leqslant 60$	10	12	$\frac{12}{10} = 1.2$
$60 < a \leqslant 90$	30	9	$\frac{9}{30} = 0.3$

Add a column for the class width.

Frequency density $= \dfrac{\text{frequency}}{\text{class width}}$

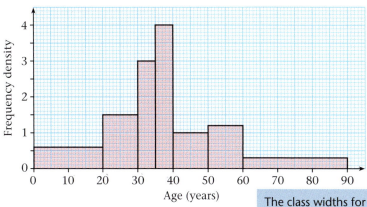

Plot frequency density on the vertical axis.

The class widths for each bar are given in the table.

(b)

The standard class interval is 5 years, so $0 < a \leqslant 20$ or 20 years is 4 lots of the standard class interval.

Age, a (years)	Class width in standard class intervals	Frequency	Frequency density
$0 < a \leqslant 20$	4	12	$\frac{12}{4} = 3$
$20 < a \leqslant 30$	2	15	$\frac{15}{2} = 7.5$
$30 < a \leqslant 35$	1	15	$\frac{15}{1} = 15$
$35 < a \leqslant 40$	1	20	$\frac{20}{1} = 20$
$40 < a \leqslant 50$	2	10	$\frac{10}{2} = 5$
$50 < a \leqslant 60$	2	12	$\frac{12}{2} = 6$
$60 < a \leqslant 90$	6	9	$\frac{9}{6} = 1.5$

$$\text{Frequency density} = \frac{\text{frequency}}{\text{class width in standard class intervals}}$$

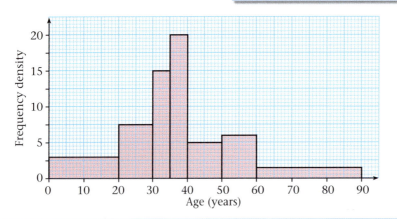

This histogram has the same shape as the histogram in part **(a)**, but the scale on the vertical axis is different.

- **Frequency** = frequency density × class width

  Frequency = frequency density × class width in standard class intervals

Example 7

The police recorded the speeds of vehicles on a motorway.
The speeds were grouped in the ranges 0 to 60 km/h, from 60 to 100 km/h and from 100 to 150 km/h.
The information is shown in this histogram.

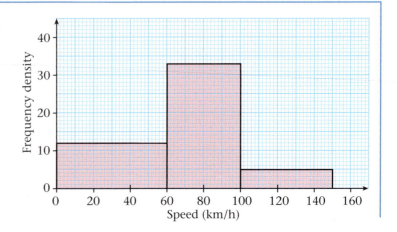

This table was used to draw the histogram.
The frequency densities were calculated using the formula

$$\text{frequency density} = \frac{\text{frequency}}{\text{class width}}$$

Speed, s (km/h)	Frequency density
$0 < s \leqslant 60$	12
$60 < s \leqslant 100$	33
$100 < s \leqslant 150$	5

(a) Work out the frequencies for each class interval.

(b) Work out the total number of vehicles in the survey.

(a) Rearranging the formula for frequency gives

frequency = frequency density × class width

Speed, s (km/h)	Class width	Frequency density	Frequency
$0 < s \leqslant 60$	60	12	12 × 60 = 720
$60 < s \leqslant 100$	40	33	33 × 40 = 1320
$100 < s \leqslant 150$	50	5	5 × 50 = 250

Add columns for class width and frequency.

(b) The total number of vehicles is the sum of the three frequencies:

720 + 1320 + 250 = 2290

Example 8

The incomplete histogram and table show some information about the salaries, in £, of the employees at Clifton Manor Hotel.

Salary, s (£)	Frequency
$0 \leqslant s < 10\,000$	4
$10\,000 \leqslant s < 15\,000$	6
$15\,000 \leqslant s < 20\,000$	
$20\,000 \leqslant s < 25\,000$	
$25\,000 \leqslant s < 30\,000$	8
$30\,000 \leqslant s < 50\,000$	4

(a) Use the histogram to complete the table.

(b) Use the table to complete the histogram.

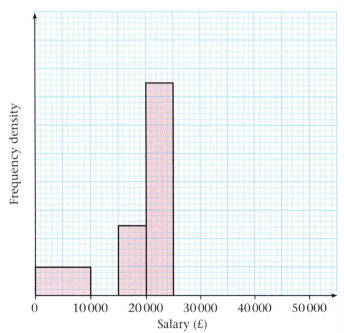

(a) From the histogram, looking at the class interval $0 \leqslant s < 10\,000$ and comparing it with the table

[ ] two squares = 4 people or [ ] = 2 people.

So from the histogram:

Class interval	Number of squares	Frequency
$15\,000 \leqslant s < 20\,000$	$2\frac{1}{2}$	$2 \times 2\frac{1}{2} = 5$
$20\,000 \leqslant s < 25\,000$	$7\frac{1}{2}$	$2 \times 7\frac{1}{2} = 15$

The completed table is:

Salary, s (£)	Frequency
$0 \leqslant s < 10\,000$	4
$10\,000 \leqslant s < 15\,000$	6
$15\,000 \leqslant s < 20\,000$	5
$20\,000 \leqslant s < 25\,000$	15
$25\,000 \leqslant s < 30\,000$	8
$30\,000 \leqslant s < 50\,000$	4

(b) Using the table, the frequency densities (in terms of number of squares) are:

Class interval	Frequency	Frequency density (number of squares)
$10\,000 \leqslant s < 15\,000$	6	$6 \div 2 = 3$
$25\,000 \leqslant s < 30\,000$	8	$8 \div 2 = 4$
$30\,000 \leqslant s < 50\,000$	4	$4 \div 2 = 2$

1 square represents 2 people. So 3 squares represent 6 people.

So the completed histogram is

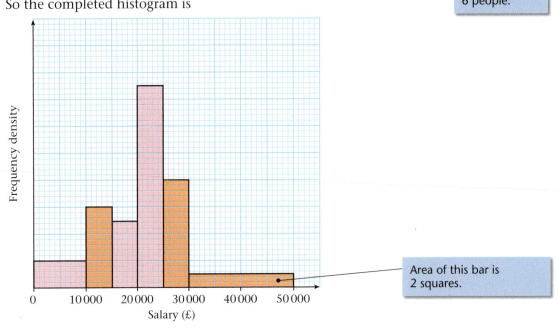

Area of this bar is 2 squares.

Exercise 2C

In these questions you may use either definition for frequency density unless told otherwise.

1 The ages of the players on a golf course are shown in the frequency table.

Age, a (years)	Frequency
$0 < a \leqslant 20$	14
$20 < a \leqslant 30$	22
$30 < a \leqslant 40$	25
$40 < a \leqslant 45$	24
$45 < a \leqslant 50$	18
$50 < a \leqslant 60$	32
$60 < a \leqslant 70$	26
$70 < a \leqslant 85$	15

Work out and tabulate the frequency densities

(a) using class widths

(b) using standard class intervals of 5 years

(c) using standard class intervals of 10 years.

2 The table shows information about the temperature, in °C, of liquids in thermos flasks in a quality control test. Draw a table to show the frequency densities.

Temperature, t (°C)	Frequency
$0 \leqslant t < 30$	12
$30 \leqslant t \leqslant 60$	59
$60 < t \leqslant 65$	15
$65 < t \leqslant 95$	15

3 400 people live in a remote South American village. Their ages are grouped and presented in the histogram.

In the histogram,

$$\text{frequency density} = \frac{\text{frequency}}{\text{class width}}$$

Use the histogram to complete a grouped frequency table like this.

Age (a) in years	Frequency density
$0 \leqslant a < 20$	
$20 \leqslant a < 30$	
$30 \leqslant a < 50$	
$50 \leqslant a < 60$	
$60 \leqslant a < 80$	
$80 \leqslant a < 90$	

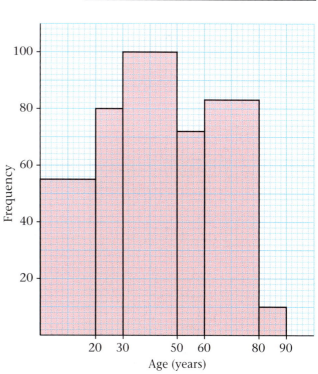

4 The weights of sharks caught by a fishing trawler are grouped and presented below in the frequency density table.
The frequency density was worked out by dividing the frequency for each group by its class width.

(a) Work out the number of sharks in each group.

(b) Work out the total number of sharks caught.

Weight, w (kg)	Frequency density
$30 < w \leqslant 40$	3.4
$40 < w \leqslant 50$	6.2
$50 < w \leqslant 55$	4.4
$55 < w \leqslant 60$	3.8
$60 < w \leqslant 85$	1.2

5 The waiting times for patients to see a doctor were recorded.
The incomplete table and histogram show some of the results.

Waiting time, t (minutes)	Frequency
$0 \leqslant t < 10$	
$10 \leqslant t < 15$	20
$15 \leqslant t < 30$	
$30 \leqslant t < 35$	5
$35 \leqslant t$	0

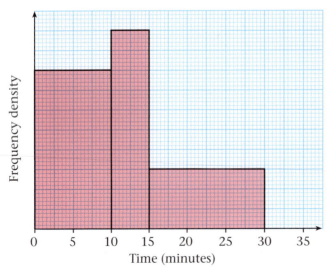

(a) Use the histogram to complete the table.

(b) Use the table to complete the histogram.

6   A sample of car owners were asked the distances, in kilometres,
    their car had travelled.
    The unfinished histogram and table show some information
    about the responses.

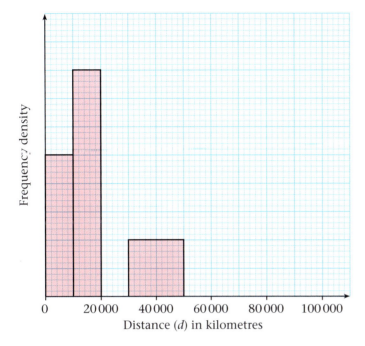

Distance, d (km)	Frequency
$0 \leqslant d < 10\,000$	25
$10\,000 \leqslant d < 20\,000$	
$20\,000 \leqslant d < 30\,000$	20
$30\,000 \leqslant d < 50\,000$	
$50\,000 \leqslant d < 100\,000$	5

(a)   Use the information in the histogram to complete the table.

(b)   Use the information in the table to complete the histogram.

Activity – Drawing histograms (an investigation)

Here are the times, in minutes, for each of 80 people to complete a Sudoku puzzle.

80	55	57	30	51	91	67	51	86	51
38	44	81	40	63	45	86	33	57	88
85	81	64	41	55	94	52	53	75	58
86	,57	35	75	74	31	53	97	61	85
40	82	50	35	72	51	85	67	36	75
56	34	51	56	37	91	50	35	52	41
58	87	45	41	94	71	76	84	76	58
47	85	49	56	46	93	60	78	47	30

1   Use the data to draw a grouped frequency table with class intervals $30 \leqslant x < 40$,
    $40 \leqslant x < 50$, etc.

2   Use the information in your grouped frequency table to draw a histogram.

3   Repeat **1** and **2** above using class intervals with a variety of (i) equal (ii) unequal widths.

4   Compare your histograms. How does the choice of class interval affect the shape of the
    distributions shown in the histograms?

Mixed exercise 2

1 The weights of 40 packages sent out by a mail order company are given in the frequency table.

Weight, w (g)	Frequency
$0 < w \leq 100$	2
$100 < w \leq 200$	8
$200 < w \leq 300$	15
$300 < w \leq 400$	10
$400 < w \leq 500$	5

Draw a frequency polygon to show this information.

2 Fifty people are asked how many miles they travelled to work. Their responses are:

8	16	22	47	51	3	12	9	12	15
18	21	32	30	17	15	17	8	9	4
13	16	11	17	52	40	14	15	22	23
21	4	10	24	16	38	12	27	11	14
20	5	9	42	57	17	8	6	32	8

Represent this information as a stem and leaf diagram.

3 As part of a project, Gary records information about the prices of two different makes of cars. His data is recorded as two frequency polygons.

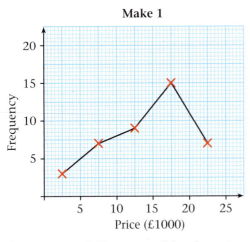

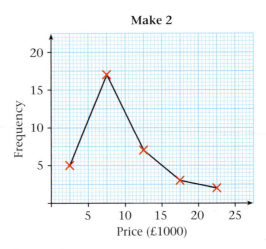

Compare, as fully as possible, the prices of the two makes of car.

4 The incomplete frequency table and histogram provide some
   information about the prices of TVs.

Price, p (£)	Frequency
$0 < p \leqslant 100$	
$100 < p \leqslant 300$	36
$300 < p \leqslant 600$	48
$600 < p \leqslant 800$	
$800 < p \leqslant 1000$	20
$1000 < p \leqslant 1500$	50

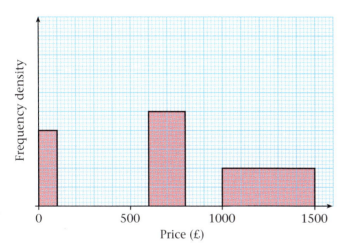

   (a) Use the information in the table to complete the histogram.

   (b) Use the histogram to complete the table.

5 The incomplete frequency table and histogram show the times
   people spent exercising one day.

Time, t (min)	Frequency
$20 < t \leqslant 25$	20
$25 < t \leqslant 40$	
$40 < t \leqslant 60$	
$60 < t \leqslant 85$	
$85 < t \leqslant 90$	6

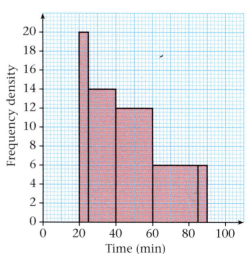

No-one spent less than 20 minutes exercising.
No-one spent more than 90 minutes
exercising.

   (a) Use the histogram to complete the table.

   (b) Work out the number of people in the survey.

6 The table and frequency polygon show information about the heights, in metres, of the mountains in the Olympus region and the Newton region of the planet Mars.

Height, h metres (in thousands)	Frequency Olympus	Frequency Newton
$0 \leqslant h < 2$		0
$2 \leqslant h < 4$		2
$4 \leqslant h < 6$		4
$6 \leqslant h < 8$		7
$8 \leqslant h < 10$		2
$10 \leqslant h < 12$		1
$12 \leqslant h < 14$		0

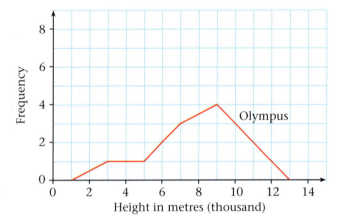

(a) Copy the table. Use the frequency polygon to complete the table.

(b) Copy the frequency polygon. Use the table to complete the frequency polygon.

(c) Comment fully on the heights of the mountains in these two regions.

7 The histogram and table show information about the number of emails received by each of the students in a school.

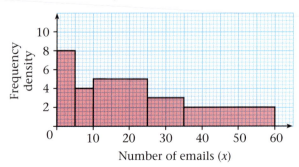

Number of emails (x)	Frequency
$0 < x \leqslant 5$	
$5 < x \leqslant 10$	20
$10 < x \leqslant 25$	
$25 < x \leqslant 35$	
$35 < x \leqslant 60$	

Copy the table.

Use the information in the histogram to complete the table.   [E]

8 A box contains some pieces of pottery from an archaeological dig.
Information about the mass of each piece of pottery is presented
in the incomplete frequency table and incomplete histogram
below.

Mass, m (g)	Frequency
$0 < m \leqslant 100$	
$100 < m \leqslant 150$	26
$150 < m \leqslant 200$	30
$200 < m \leqslant 250$	
$250 < m \leqslant 400$	12

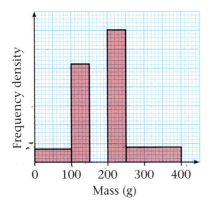

(a) Use the histogram to complete the table.

(b) Use the table to complete the histogram.

(c) Work out the number of pieces of pottery in the box.

(d) A piece of pottery is selected at random from the box.
Work out the probability that this piece of pottery will weigh
over 200 g.

9 The incomplete frequency table and histogram below provide information about the distribution of ages of the people living in Medina.

Age, a (years)	Frequency
$0 < a \leqslant 15$	20
$15 < a \leqslant 20$	
$20 < a \leqslant 30$	42
$30 < a \leqslant 40$	
$40 < a \leqslant 65$	57
$65 < a \leqslant 70$	24
$70 < a \leqslant 90$	18

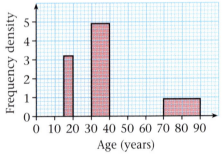

(a) Copy and complete the table.

(b) Copy and complete the histogram.

(c) Find the total number of people who live in Medina.

(d) Estimate the number of people living in Medina who are aged between 25 and 40. Give your reasons.

10 Alan is doing a survey of the heights of boys and girls in Year 7. He first takes a random sample of 70 boys from Year 7.

(a) Suggest a suitable method that Alan could use to take a random sample.

The frequency table and the incomplete histogram show information about the boys' heights in this sample of 70 boys.

Height of boys, h (cm)	Frequency
$140 \leqslant h < 145$	10
$145 \leqslant h < 148$	15
$148 \leqslant h < 150$	20
$150 \leqslant h < 154$	16
$154 \leqslant h < 157$	9

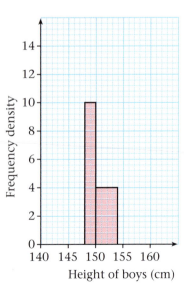

(b) Use the information in the table to complete the histogram.

Alan then takes a random sample of 70 girls from Year 7. The histogram and the incomplete frequency table show information about the girls' heights in this sample of 70 girls.

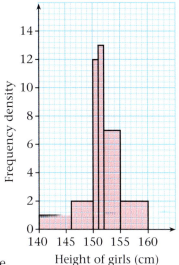

Height of girls, h (cm)	Frequency
$140 \leqslant h < 146$	
$146 \leqslant h < 150$	
$150 \leqslant h < 151$	
$151 \leqslant h < 152$	13
$152 \leqslant h < 155$	21
$155 \leqslant h < 160$	

(c) Use the information in the histogram to complete the table.

(d) Use both tables and both histograms to give **two** differences between the distributions of boys' heights and girls' heights.

[E]

11 The weights of some babies are given in the frequency table.

Weight, w (kg)	Frequency
$0 \leqslant w < 2$	0
$2 \leqslant w < 2.5$	8
$2.5 \leqslant w < 3$	9
$3 \leqslant w < 4$	15
$4 \leqslant w < 6$	27
$w \geqslant 6$	0

Draw a histogram to show the distribution of weights of the babies.

Use a scale of 2 cm to 1 kg on the weight axis.   [E]

12 The incomplete frequency table and histogram provide some information about the speeds of runners in a marathon. Complete the table and histogram.

Speed, s (m/s)	Frequency
$0 < s \leqslant 3$	
$3 < s \leqslant 4$	30
$4 < s \leqslant 5$	
$5 < s \leqslant 6$	40
$6 < s \leqslant 8$	
$8 < s \leqslant 10$	10

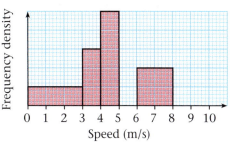

13 The histogram shows information about the examination marks
of some candidates.

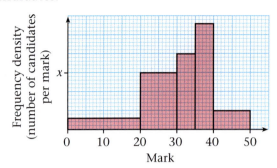

150 candidates scored a mark greater than or equal to 20 and less
than 30.

(a) Find the value of x.

The pass mark for the examination was 31.

(b) 'Exactly half the candidates passed.'
Do you agree or disagree with this statement?
Justify your answer.

Summary of key points

1 A **pie chart** shows how data is shared or divided into different
categories.

2 A **stem and leaf diagram** shows the shape of the distribution and
keeps all the data values. It needs a **key** to show how the stem and
leaf are combined.

3 A **histogram** is used to display continuous grouped data.

4 A **frequency polygon** shows the general pattern of data
represented by a histogram.

5 In a histogram the **area** of each rectangular bar represents the
frequency for that class interval.

6 In a histogram with unequal class intervals, the vertical axis shows
frequency density.

7 Frequency density $= \dfrac{\text{frequency}}{\text{class width}}$

Frequency density $= \dfrac{\text{frequency}}{\text{class width in standard class intervals}}$

8 Frequency $=$ frequency density $\times$ class width
Frequency $=$ frequency density $\times$ class width in standard class
intervals

3 Averages and spread

- The **mode** of a set of data is the value which occurs most often.

20 Introducing the median

- The **median** is the middle value when the data are arranged in order of size. For n data values, the median is the $\frac{n+1}{2}$th value when the data are arranged in order.

- The **mean** of a set of data is the sum of the values divided by the number of values:

$$\text{mean} = \frac{\text{sum of values}}{\text{number of values}}$$

- The **range** of a set of data is the difference between the highest value and the lowest value: range = highest value − lowest value

- For a frequency distribution: mean $= \dfrac{\Sigma fx}{\Sigma f}$

3.1 Stem and leaf diagrams and frequency distributions

Example 1

The stem and leaf diagram shows the number of injections given by a nurse on each of 20 days.

```
0 | 3, 4, 4, 6, 9
1 | 0, 1, 2, 3, 3, 7, 7, 9        11th value
2 | 1, 1, 7, 7, 7, 7
3 | 1
```

10th value

Key: 3|1 means 31 injections

(a) Find the mode.

(b) Find the median.

(c) Work out the range.

(a) The mode is 27.

The mode is the value which occurs most often.

(b) The median is the $\frac{20+1}{2} = 10.5$th value $= 15$

The average of the 10th and 11th values is $\frac{13+17}{2} = 15$

(c) The range is $31 - 3 = 28$

Example 2

In a survey, Helga recorded the number of cups of tea that each of her friends drank one particular weekend.
Her results are shown in the table.

Work out

(a) the mode

(b) the median

(c) the mean.

Number of cups, x	Frequency, f
0	6
1	14
2	10
3	5
	Total 35

More than 135 million cups of tea are drunk in Britain each day.

> In the frequency table the mode is the item of data with the highest frequency.

(a) The highest frequency is 14, for 1 cup of tea.
The mode is 1 cup of tea.

(b) There are 35 people altogether. The data in the table are in order.

The middle person is the $\frac{35 + 1}{2}$ = 18th person.

The 18th person in the table drank 1 cup of tea.
The median is 1 cup of tea.

Number of cups, x	Frequency f	
0	6 •	First 6 people
1	14 •	7th–20th people 18th person is in this group.

(c)

Number of cups, x	Frequency, f	Frequency × number of cups, f × x
0	6	0
1	14	14
2	10	20
3	5	15
	$\Sigma f = 35$	$\Sigma fx = 49$

> Σf = the sum of all the f values.

The mean $= \dfrac{\Sigma fx}{\Sigma f}$

$= \frac{49}{35} = 1.4$ cups of tea per person.

- When the data are arranged in ascending order,
  - the **lower quartile** is the value one quarter of the way into the data. For n data values, the lower quartile is the $\frac{1}{4}(n + 1)$th value.
  - the **upper quartile** is the value three quarters of the way into the data. For n data values, the upper quartile is the $\frac{3}{4}(n + 1)$th value.
  - the **interquartile range** = upper quartile − lower quartile.

20 The median and quartiles

Example 3

The stem and leaf diagram shows the numbers of people on each of 23 buses.

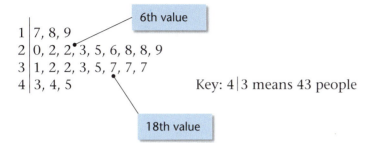

1 | 7, 8, 9
2 | 0, 2, 2, 3, 5, 6, 8, 8, 9
3 | 1, 2, 2, 3, 5, 7, 7, 7
4 | 3, 4, 5

6th value

18th value

Key: 4|3 means 43 people

(a) Find the lower quartile.

(b) Find the upper quartile.

(c) Find the interquartile range.

(a) The lower quartile is the $\frac{1}{4}(23 + 1)) = $ 6th value = 22

(b) The upper quartile is the $\frac{3}{4}(23 + 1) = $ 18th value = 37

(c) The interquartile range = upper quartile − lower quartile
$$= 37 − 22 = 15$$

Example 4

The table shows information about 31 students' test marks.

Mark	5	6	7	8	9	10
Frequency	2	4	5	10	7	3

Work out

(a) the range

(b) the interquartile range.

(a) Range = highest mark − lowest mark = 10 − 5 = 5 marks

(b) Interquartile range = upper quartile − lower quartile
The marks are in order, so the lower quartile is the $\frac{1}{4}(31 + 1) = $ 8th value = 7 marks
The upper quartile is the $\frac{3}{4}(31 + 1) = $ 24th value = 9 marks
So the interquartile range = 9 − 7 = 2 marks

Exercise 3A

1   The table shows information about the number of goals scored by
    Halifax Wanderers in each of 20 matches.

Number of goals, x	Frequency, f
0	5
1	6
2	7
3	1
4	1
	Total 20

Work out

(a) the mode

(b) the median

(c) the mean.

2   The stem and leaf diagram shows information about the areas of
    32 photographs.

```
0 | 8, 8, 9
1 | 1, 1, 3, 4, 4, 8, 9
2 | 0, 3, 5, 5, 7, 8, 8, 9
3 | 2, 2, 3, 3, 5, 6, 8, 8
4 | 1, 1, 3, 3, 5, 8          Key: 4|1 represents 41 cm²
```

(a) Write down the number of photographs that have an area of
     38 cm^2.

(b) Work out the median.   [E]

3   The stem and leaf diagram shows the numbers of space satellites
    launched by each of 27 countries in the last ten years.

```
2 | 4, 7, 8
3 | 1, 3, 5, 5, 6, 8, 8, 9
4 | 0, 1, 2, 3, 5, 7, 7, 7, 8, 8
5 | 1, 1, 3, 4, 5, 7          Key: 8|1 means 81
```

Work out

(a) the median

(b) the range

(c) the interquartile range.   [E]

4 The table shows information about the number of days lost through illness in April for each of 47 employees in a company.

Days	0	1	2	3	4
Frequency	27	9	6	3	2

Work out

(a) the range

(b) the interquartile range.

5 Use the 'mean' function on your calculator to work out the mean of the numbers

     3, 7, 8, 5, 9, 10, 7, 8, 6, 2.

Check your result without using a calculator.

The key may be labelled X or $\bar{x}$.

6 In a survey, Ross records the number of swimming certificates people have. The table shows his results.

Certificates	0	1	2	3	4	5
Frequency	10	15	11	9	4	1

Work out

(a) the mode

(b) the mean

(c) the interquartile range.

7 The table shows information about the number of people living in 100 households.

Number of people, x	Frequency, f
1	5
2	13
3	20
4	25
5	19
6	11
7	7
	$\Sigma f = 100$

Work out

(a) the mode

(b) the mean

(c) the range.

3.2 Grouped frequency distributions

- For grouped data, the **modal class** is the group that has the highest frequency.
- For large data sets ($n \geqslant 50$) the median is the $\frac{n}{2}$th value.
- For grouped data you can find the class interval that contains the median.
- For a grouped frequency distribution

  mean $= \dfrac{\sum fx}{\sum f}$ where the x values are the mid-points of the class intervals.

Example 5

The ages of 50 members of a squash club are given in the table.

Age, a (years)	Frequency
$10 < a \leqslant 20$	4
$20 < a \leqslant 30$	18
$30 < a \leqslant 40$	10
$40 < a \leqslant 50$	15
$50 < a \leqslant 60$	3

(a) Write down the modal class interval for the ages.

(b) Write down the class interval containing the median age.

(c) Work out an estimate for the mean of the ages.

(d) Work out the maximum possible range for the ages.

The badminton club has 50 members. The mean of their ages is 25 years.

(e) Explain why it is not possible to say that on the whole the members of the badminton club are younger than the members of the squash club. You may illustrate your answer with an example.

(a) The interval with the highest frequency is $20 < a \leqslant 30$. This is the modal class interval.

(b) There are 50 members in total.
The median is the $\frac{50}{2} = 25$th person.
The class interval containing the median is $30 < a \leqslant 40$.

> There are 22 people $\leqslant$ 30 years.
> The 25th person is in the interval $30 < a \leqslant 40$.

(c)

Age, a (years)	Mid-point, x	Frequency, f	$f \times x$
$10 < a \leqslant 20$	15	4	$4 \times 15 = \quad 60$
$20 < a \leqslant 30$	25	18	$18 \times 25 = \quad 450$
$30 < a \leqslant 40$	35	10	$10 \times 35 = \quad 350$
$40 < a \leqslant 50$	45	15	$15 \times 45 = \quad 675$
$50 < a \leqslant 60$	55	3	$3 \times 55 = \quad 165$
		$\Sigma f = 50$	$\Sigma fx = 1700$

You do not know the exact data values. To estimate the mean, you can use the mid-point of each interval.

So the estimated mean age is $\frac{1700}{50} = 34$ years.

(d) The range of the ages = oldest age − youngest age. The youngest could be (just over) 10 years and the oldest could be 60. So the maximum possible range is $60 - 10 = 50$ years.

You do not know the exact oldest and youngest ages.

(e) The mean age of the badminton club is lower than the mean age of the squash club, so it might look as if the badminton players are younger, on the whole. However, we do not have the range of ages for the badminton club, so we simply cannot arrive at any sensible comparison.

For example the 50 badminton club members could be

20 aged 10 and 30 aged 35

This gives a mean age of
$$\frac{20 \times 10 + 30 \times 35}{50} = \frac{1250}{50} = 25$$
But for this group it would be silly to say that the badminton club are, in general, younger than the squash club, as 30 (over half) of them are older than the mean age of the squash club.

Exercise 3B

1 Bill recorded the times, in minutes, taken to complete his last 40 homeworks.
This table shows information about the times.

Weight, t (minutes)	Frequency	
$20 < t \leqslant 25$	8	
$25 < t \leqslant 30$	3	
$30 < t \leqslant 35$	7	
$35 < t \leqslant 40$	7	
$40 < t \leqslant 45$	15	

(a) Find the class interval in which the median lies.

(b) Calculate an estimate of the mean time it took Bill to complete each homework.　　　　[E]

2 The speeds of 80 vehicles on a main road at lunchtime are recorded in the table.

Speed, s (mph)	Frequency
$0 < s \leqslant 10$	1
$10 < s \leqslant 20$	2
$20 < s \leqslant 30$	10
$30 < s \leqslant 40$	30
$40 < s \leqslant 50$	32
$50 < s \leqslant 60$	3
$60 < s \leqslant 70$	2

(a) Work out an estimate of the mean speed of these vehicles.

(b) Write down the modal class interval for the speed.

(c) Write down the class interval which contains the median.

The speed limit on the road is 45 mph.

(d) Estimate how many of the vehicles in the survey were exceeding the speed limit. Give your reasons.

A second survey was conducted on the same road at midnight. For this second survey the mean speed of the vehicles was found to be 43 mph. A report on the two surveys concluded that

'on the whole people tend to drive faster at midnight than at lunchtime'.

(e) Comment on the correctness or otherwise of this conclusion.

3 The distances, in light years, to the stars in a constellation, are shown in the table.

Distance, d (light years)	Frequency
$5 < d \leqslant 10$	3
$10 < d \leqslant 20$	13
$20 < d \leqslant 30$	23
$30 < d \leqslant 50$	7
$50 < d \leqslant 100$	5

The stars in the night sky are divided into 88 constellations. This photo shows the Horsehead Nebula in the constellation Orion.

(a) Write down the modal class interval for the distances.

(b) Write down the class interval containing the median.

(c) Work out an estimate for the mean of the distances.

(d) Work out the maximum possible range of the distances.

The average distance to the stars in another constellation is 25.1 light years.

(e) Explain why it is not possible to say that on the whole the stars in the second constellation are nearer than the stars in the first constellation.

3.3 Cumulative frequency diagrams and box plots

20 Introducing box plots
20 Box plots from cumulative frequency diagrams

- The largest possible value in an interval is called the **upper class boundary**.
- **Cumulative frequency** is the total frequency up to a particular class boundary.
- To draw a **cumulative frequency diagram**, plot the cumulative frequency against the upper class boundary of each interval. Draw a curve through the points.
- For a cumulative frequency diagram:
  - The **median** is the value half way into the distribution
  - The **lower quartile** is the value one quarter of the way into the distribution
  - The **upper quartile** is the value three quarters of the way into the distribution
  - **Interquartile range** = upper quartile − lower quartile.
- To draw a **box plot** you need five pieces of information:
  - the lowest value
  - the lower quartile
  - the median
  - the upper quartile
  - the highest value.

Example 6

There are 150 members of Vijay's sports club. The ages of the members are grouped and set out in this table.

Age, a (years)	Frequency
$0 < a \leqslant 10$	6
$10 < a \leqslant 20$	20
$20 < a \leqslant 30$	24
$30 < a \leqslant 40$	33
$40 < a \leqslant 50$	28
$50 < a \leqslant 60$	22
$60 < a \leqslant 70$	12
$70 < a \leqslant 80$	5

(a) Construct a cumulative frequency table.
(b) Draw the cumulative frequency curve.
(c) Use the curve to estimate the median age of the members.

(d) Use the curve to estimate the interquartile range of the ages.

(e) Estimate the percentage of members aged between 23 and 46 years.

(f) Construct a box plot for this distribution.

(a) The cumulative frequency table is

Upper class boundary	Cumulative frequency
10	6
20	26
30	50
40	83
50	111
60	133
70	145
80	150

> 6 from $0 < a \leqslant 10$ plus 20 from $10 < a \leqslant 20$.

> This includes all the people aged up to and including 50.

(b) The cumulative frequency curve is

> For large data sets, use $\frac{3}{4}n$ and $\frac{1}{4}n$ for the upper and lower quartiles.

> Upper quartile $\frac{3}{4} \times 150 = 112.5$th value.

> Median $\frac{1}{2} \times 150 = 75$th value.

> Lower quartile $= \frac{1}{4} \times 150 = 37.5$th value.

> Plot the upper class boundaries 10, 20, 30, ... against the cumulative frequencies.

> Upper quartile = 50

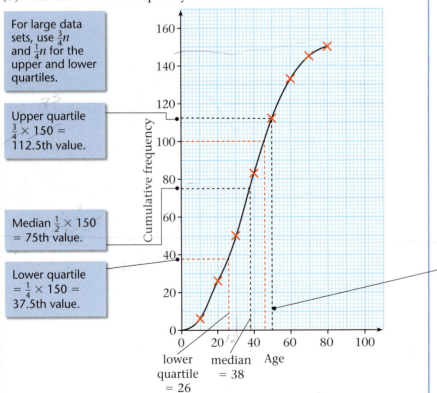

lower quartile = 26   median = 38   Age

(c) From the curve the estimate of the median age is 38 years.

(d) Upper quartile = 50
Lower quartile = 26
So interquartile range = 50 − 26 = 24 years.

(e) From the graph the estimates are

32 members aged up to 23
102 members aged up to 46

So the estimate for the number of members aged between 23 and 46 is

102 − 32 = 70

70 as a percentage of 150 is

$\frac{70}{150} \times 100 = 46\frac{2}{3}\%$

(f) The box plot for the distribution is

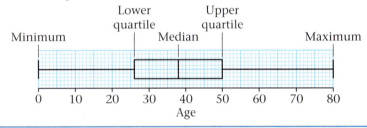

Exercise 3C

1 75 people took part in a darts competition. They each threw darts until they hit a bullseye. The numbers of darts thrown before scoring a bullseye are grouped in the frequency table.

Number of darts thrown	Frequency
1 to 5	10
6 to 10	17
11 to 15	11
16 to 20	5
21 to 25	12
26 to 30	20

The bullseye on a standard darts board has a radius of 5 mm.

(a) Construct a cumulative frequency table.

(b) Draw a cumulative frequency curve.

(c) Use your cumulative frequency curve to find estimates for
  (i) the median number of darts thrown
  (ii) the upper and lower quartiles for the number of darts thrown
  (iii) the interquartile range of the number of darts thrown
  (iv) the proportion of people who took between 12 and 24 darts to hit a bullseye.

(d) Draw a box plot for this distribution.

2 A dentist's receptionist recorded the lengths of time that 80 patients had to wait before being checked in. The waiting times were as follows.

Waiting time (t) seconds	Frequency
$0 < t \leqslant 60$	4
$60 < t \leqslant 120$	8
$120 < t \leqslant 180$	10
$180 < t \leqslant 240$	18
$240 < t \leqslant 300$	30
$300 < t \leqslant 360$	10

(a) Construct a cumulative frequency table.

(b) Draw a cumulative frequency curve.

(c) Use the curve to estimate
   (i) the median waiting time
   (ii) the interquartile range of the waiting times.

(d) Draw a box plot for the waiting times.

3.4 Comparing distributions

Example 7

Sally has collected data on the heights of 50 boys and 50 girls.
Some of her results are represented on the joint cumulative frequency diagram below.

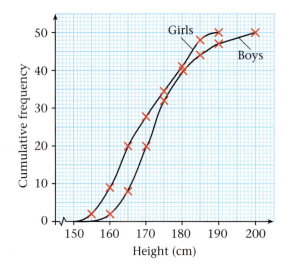

(a) Make **three** valid statistical conclusions based on these graphs. Give your reasons in each case.

(b) Work out an estimate of the percentage of girls taller than
  (i) the median height for the boys
 (ii) the upper quartile of the boys' heights
(iii) the 90th percentile of the boys' heights.

(a) Three valid conclusions are:
  - In general the girls are not as tall as the boys. This is shown by the cumulative frequency curve for the girls, which is to the left of that for the boys.
  - The range of boys' heights is greater than the range of girls' heights.
    The range of heights for the girls is 190 − 150 = 40 cm.
    The range for the boys is 200 − 150 − 50 cm.
  - Median height for girls is 168 cm.
    Median height for boys is 172 cm.
    So the median height for the boys is greater than the median height for the girls.

> These are estimated from the cumulative frequency curve.

(b) **(i)** The median height for the boys is 172 cm.
From the girls' cumulative frequency diagram, 30 girls are 172 cm or less.
So 50 − 30 = 20 girls are taller than the boys' median height.
As a percentage, $\frac{20}{50}$ = 40%.
40% of the girls are taller than the median height for the boys.

> See the blue dashed line on the graph.

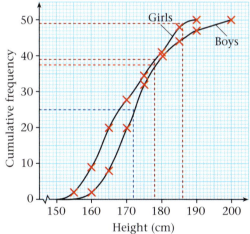

  (ii) From the graph, the upper quartile of the boys' heights is the 37.5th value = 178 cm.
From the girls' curve, 39 girls are 178 cm or less.
So 50 − 39 = 11 girls are taller than 178 cm.
As a percentage $\frac{11}{50}$ = 22%.
22% of the girls are taller than the upper quartile for the boys.

  (iii) The 90th percentile for the boys is 186 cm.
50 − 49 = 1 girl is taller than 186 cm.
So $\frac{1}{50}$ = 2% of the girls are taller than the 90th percentile of the boys' heights.

> The 90th percentile is the height below which 90% × 50 = 45 boys' heights lie.

• To compare the information in two or more box plots, draw the diagrams next to each other.

20 Comparing box plots

Example 8

Here is the box plot for Vijay's sports club, from Example 6.

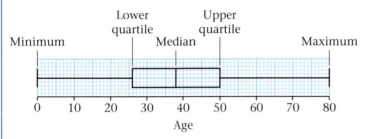

The median age of the members of Tina's sports club is 43 years. The upper and lower quartiles of the ages at Tina's sports club are 58 and 20 years respectively.

The maximum age is 78 and the minimum age is 6.

Compare as fully as possible the distribution of ages at the two sports clubs.

Comparing the two distributions using box plots:

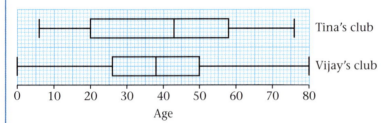

The median age at Tina's club is greater than the median age at Vijay's. However the interquartile range at Tina's is greater than that at Vijay's.

This means that there could be a significant number of members at Tina's club younger than the lower quartile age at Vijay's club, or many more older than the upper quartile age at Vijay's club.

So you cannot make any definite statement about which club has the older membership overall.

Exercise 3D

1 The grouped frequency table at the top of the next page gives information about the weekly rainfall at Gatwick airport during the year 2005.

(a) Construct a cumulative frequency table.

(b) Draw a cumulative frequency curve.

(c) Estimate the median weekly rainfall at Gatwick airport during 2005.

(d) Estimate the interquartile range of the rainfall.

(e) Estimate the number of weeks during 2005 when the weekly rainfall at Gatwick airport was greater than 15 mm.

During 2005 the weekly rainfall at Manchester airport had a median of 22 mm with upper and lower quartiles of 9 mm and 30 mm.

(f) Comment as fully as possible about the difference in weekly rainfall at the two airports during 2005.

Weekly rainfall, r (mm)	Frequency
$0 < r \leqslant 10$	18
$10 < r \leqslant 20$	20
$20 < r \leqslant 30$	6
$30 < r \leqslant 40$	3
$40 < r \leqslant 50$	3
$50 < r \leqslant 60$	2

2 The joint cumulative frequency diagram represents the weights of 80 girls and 80 boys.

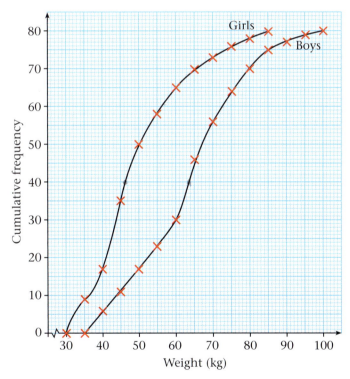

(a) Make three valid statistical comparisons based on the diagram.

(b) Draw parallel box plots for the two distributions.

(c) Work out an estimate for the percentage of girls that are

    (i) heavier than the upper quartile weight for the boys

    (ii) lighter than the lower 15th percentile of the weight for the boys.

3 A group of 80 students took an examination in Science and an examination in Geography. Both examinations had a total of 100 marks.
The diagrams below represent the box plots for the distribution of marks.

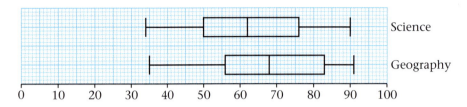

Comment as fully as possible on the relative difficulty of these two examinations.

Activity – Comparing the performance of male and female athletes

The spreadsheet shows information about the winners of the 100 m sprint in the Olympic Games from 1948 to 2004.

	A	B	C	D	E
1		**Men**		**Women**	
2	Year	Athlete	Time (s)	Athlete	Time (s)
3	1948	Harrison Dillard	10.3	Fanny Blankers-Koen	11.9
4	1952	Lindy Remigino	10.4	Marjorie Jackson	11.5
5	1956	Bobby Morrow	10.5	Betty Cuthbert	11.5
6	1960	Armin Hary	10.2	Wilma Rudolph	11
7	1964	Bob Hayes	10	Wyomia Tyus	11.4
8	1968	Jim Hines	9.95	Wyomia Tyus	11
9	1972	Valery Borov	10.14	Renate Stecher	11.07
10	1976	Hasely Crawford	10.06	Annegret Richter	11.08
11	1980	Allan Wells	10.25	Lyudmila Konratyeva	11.06
12	1984	Carl Lewis	9.99	Evelyn Ashford	10.97
13	1988	Carl Lewis	9.92	Florence Griffith-Joyner	10.54
14	1992	Linford Christie	9.96	Gail Devers	10.82
15	1996	Donovan Bailey	9.84	Gail Devers	10.94
16	2000	Maurice Greene	9.87	Marion Jones	10.75
17	2004	Justin Gatlin	9.85	Yuliya Nesterenko	10.93

1 Draw box plots to compare the times for male and female athletes.
2 Comment fully on the difference in performance of male and female athletes in this event.
3 Investigate the performance of male and female athletes in the Olympic Games for a different event.

Mixed exercise 3

1 A company tested 100 batteries.

The table shows information about the number of hours that the batteries lasted.

Time (t) hours	Frequency
$50 \leqslant t < 55$	12
$55 \leqslant t < 60$	21
$60 \leqslant t < 65$	36
$65 \leqslant t < 70$	23
$70 \leqslant t < 75$	8

(a) Copy and complete the cumulative frequency table for this information.

Time (t) hours	Cumulative frequency
$50 \leqslant t < 55$	12
$50 \leqslant t < 60$	
$50 \leqslant t < 65$	
$50 \leqslant t < 70$	
$50 \leqslant t < 75$	

(b) Draw a cumulative frequency graph for your completed table.

(c) Use you graph to find an estimate for the median time.
You must state the units of your answer.   [E]

2 An anthropologist recorded the heights, in cm, of the people in each of two villages. The results are summarised in the box plots.

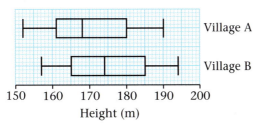

Comment as fully as possible on the comparison in height between people in these two villages.

3 The mean weekly wage at Spencer plc is £210.
The mean weekly wage at Creswell Ltd is £250.
Is it fair to say that the people at Creswell Ltd are better paid than the people at Spencer plc? Explain your answer.

4 The cumulative frequency curves below provide information on average house prices in the UK in 1995 and 2005.

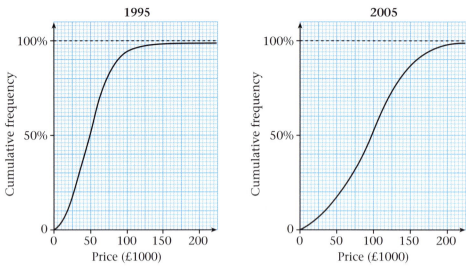

Comment as fully as possible on the variations of average house prices between 1995 and 2005. Your comments must be supported by statistical evidence.

5 75 people took part in a general knowledge quiz with a maximum possible mark of 30.
The numbers of marks are grouped in the frequency table.

Marks	Number of people
1–5	10
6–10	15
11–15	14
16–20	7
21–25	9
26–30	20

(a) Write down the modal class interval.

(b) Work out the class interval which contains the median.

(c) Work out an estimate for the mean number of marks.

6 The diagram below represents a box plot for the distribution of ages of people on a world cruise.
A total of 400 people are on the cruise.
Sketch the cumulative frequency curve for the ages of the people on the cruise.

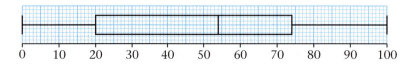

7 A biologist recorded the amount of lead, in parts per million (ppm), in 80 samples of water from a river.

Lead, l (ppm)	Frequency
$0 < l \leqslant 100$	4
$100 < l \leqslant 200$	15
$200 < l \leqslant 300$	36
$300 < l \leqslant 400$	20
$400 < l \leqslant 500$	5

(a) Write down the modal class for this distribution.

(b) Represent the distribution using a frequency polygon.

(c) Work out an estimate for the mean amount of lead in the samples.

(d) Draw the cumulative frequency curve for this distribution.

(e) Use your cumulative frequency curve to find an estimate for
   (i) the median amount of lead in the samples
   (ii) the interquartile range of the amounts of lead in the samples.

(f) Draw the box plot for this distribution.

8 The police conduct a survey of the speeds of 120 vehicles using a main road. Information about the results of the survey is given in the table.

Speed, s (mph)	Frequency
$0 < s \leqslant 10$	2
$10 < s \leqslant 20$	18
$20 < s \leqslant 30$	24
$30 < s \leqslant 40$	38
$40 < s \leqslant 50$	17
$50 < s \leqslant 60$	10
$60 < s \leqslant 70$	8
$70 < s \leqslant 80$	3

(a) Represent this distribution using a frequency polygon.

(b) Write down the modal class interval.

(c) Work out an estimate for the mean speed of these vehicles.

(d) Draw the cumulative frequency curve for the distribution.

(e) Use your cumulative frequency curve to find estimates for
   (i) the median speed of these vehicles
   (ii) the interquartile range of the speeds
   (iii) the number of vehicles exceeding a speed of 55 mph.

(f) Draw a box plot for the distribution.

9 The diagrams below represent three frequency distributions.

(a) 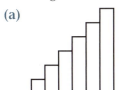   (b) 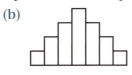   (c)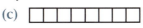

Sketch the cumulative frequency curve for each distribution.

10 The table provides information about the cruising speeds of 120 aircraft.

Speed, s (mph)	Frequency
$200 < s \leqslant 300$	14
$300 < s \leqslant 400$	22
$400 < s \leqslant 500$	36
$500 < s \leqslant 600$	25
$600 < s \leqslant 700$	16
$700 < s \leqslant 800$	7

(a) Work out an estimate of the mean speed.

(b) Draw the frequency polygon.

(c) Complete a cumulative frequency table.

(d) Draw the cumulative frequency curve.

(e) Find an estimate of the median speed.

(f) Find estimates for
  (i) the lower quartile speed
  (ii) the upper quartile speed
  (iii) the interquartile range of speeds.

(g) Draw the box plot for this distribution.

11 Sketch the histogram for this cumulative frequency curve, using equal class intervals.

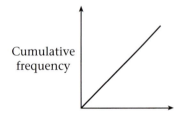

12 Here are four cumulative frequency diagrams.

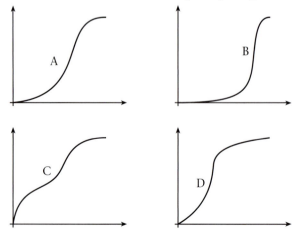

Here are four box plots.

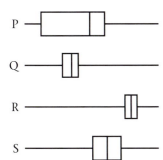

Match each box plot to a cumulative frequency diagram.   [E]

Summary of key points

1 The **mode** of a set of data is the value which occurs most often.

2 The **median** is the middle value when the data are arranged in order of size. For n data values, the median is the $\frac{n+1}{2}$th value when the data are arranged in order.

3 The **mean** of a set of data is the sum of the values divided by the number of values:

$$\text{mean} = \frac{\text{sum of values}}{\text{number of values}}$$

4 The **range** of a set of data is the difference between the highest value and the lowest value: range = highest value − lowest value

5 For a frequency distribution: $\text{mean} = \dfrac{\Sigma fx}{\Sigma f}$

6 When the data are arranged in ascending order:
   ○ the **lower quartile** is the value one quarter of the way into the data. For n data values, the lower quartile is the $\frac{1}{4}(n+1)$th value.
   ○ the **upper quartile** is the value three quarters of the way into the data. For n data values, the upper quartile is the $\frac{3}{4}(n+1)$th value.
   ○ the **interquartile range** = upper quartile − lower quartile.

7 For grouped data, the **modal class** is the group that has the highest frequency.

8 For large data sets ($n \geqslant 50$) the median is the $\frac{n}{2}$th value.

9 For grouped data you can find the class interval that contains the median.

10 For a grouped frequency distribution
   $$\text{mean} = \frac{\Sigma fx}{\Sigma f}$$
   where the x values are the mid-points of the class intervals.

11 The largest possible value in an interval is called the **upper class boundary**.

12 **Cumulative frequency** is the total frequency up to a particular class boundary.

13 To draw a **cumulative frequency diagram**, plot the cumulative frequency against the upper class boundary of each interval. Draw a curve through the points.

14 For a cumulative frequency graph:
  ○ The **median** is the value half way into the distribution
  ○ The **lower quartile** is the value one quarter of the way into the distribution
  ○ The **upper quartile** is the value three quarters of the way into the distribution
  ○ **Interquartile range** = upper quartile − lower quartile.

15 To draw a **box plot** you need five pieces of information:
  ○ the lowest value   ○ the lower quartile
  ○ the median   ○ the upper quartile
  ○ the highest value.

16 To compare the information in two or more box plots, draw the diagrams next to each other.

4 Relationships and trends in data

4.1 Scatter graphs and correlation

20 Plotting scatter diagrams

- A linear relationship between two sets of data is called a **correlation**.

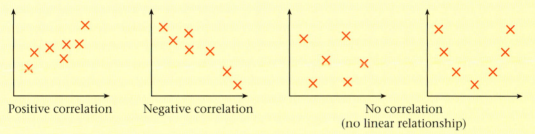

Positive correlation   Negative correlation   No correlation
(no linear relationship)

- The **line of best fit** is a straight line that passes through or as close to as many of the plotted points as possible.
- A line of best fit gives a model for how two variables are related. The closer the plotted points are to the line, the better the correlation.
- A line of best fit can be used to estimate other data values within the range of the data given.
- The equation of the line of best fit has the form $y = mx + c$, where m is the gradient and c is the intercept with the y-axis.

> You cannot be sure that the pattern continues outside this range.

Example 1

The table provides information about the ages and values of ten used cars.

Age (years)	Value (£1000)
3	5.5
6	2.4
8	1.3
2	8
2	7.5
8	10
4	4.6
5	4
6	3.9
1	9

(a) Plot these points on a scatter graph.

(b) Comment on the relationship between the ages and the values of the cars.

(c) Draw a line of best fit.

(d) Use your line of best fit to
      (i) estimate the value of a car aged 7 years
      (ii) estimate the age of a car valued at £7200.

(a) (i)

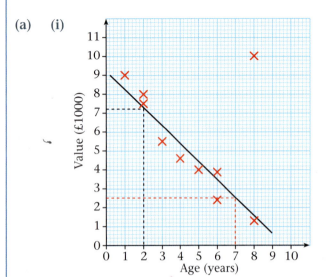

When drawing the line of best fit, the car at (8, 10) was ignored. This point is so far from the other data points it is treated as an exception. It could, for example, be a luxury car.

There are roughly equal numbers of points either side of the line of best fit.

The data points are close to the line of best fit. This shows there is a good correlation between the age of a car and its value.

(b) The scatter graph shows negative correlation. On the whole, the older the car the lower its value.

(d)   (i) Estimate for the value of a car aged 7 years = £2500.
     (ii) Estimate for the age of a car valued at £7200 = 2 years.

Example 2

A line of best fit has been drawn on this scatter graph.
Work out the equation of the line of best fit.

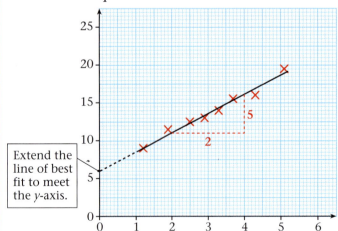

Extend the line of best fit to meet the y-axis.

The gradient of the line of best fit is $\frac{5}{2} = 2.5$

The equation of a line has the form $y = mx + c$, where m is the gradient and c is the y-intercept.
Here $m = \frac{5}{2} = 2.5$ and $c = 7$.
So the equation of the line of best fit is $y = 2.5x + 7$.

Exercise 4A

1 The table shows the units of electricity and the units of gas used in a factory over ten days.

Gas	26	41	40	39	44	41	25	40	33	37
Electricity	20	39	38	40	40	39	28	44	30	39

(a) Plot these points on a scatter graph.

(b) Draw the line of best fit.

(c) Comment on the correlation between gas and electricity use.

(d) On the next day 36 units of gas are used. Estimate the likely number of units of electricity used.

2 The scatter graph shows the Science mark and the Maths mark for 15 students.

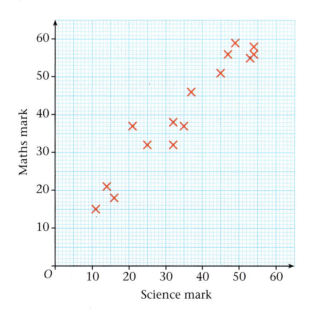

(a) What type of correlation does this scatter graph show?

(b) Copy the scatter graph. Draw a line of best fit.

Sophie's Science mark was 42.

(c) Use your line of best fit to estimate Sophie's Maths mark.   [E]

3 Here is a scatter graph.

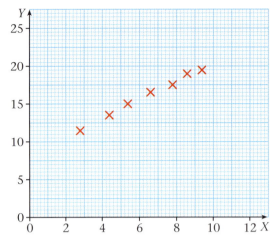

(a) Comment on the correlation between X and Y.

(b) Copy the scatter graph and draw the line of best fit.

(c) Work out the equation of the line of best fit.

Activity – Do taller people have bigger feet?

1 Collect data for your class.

2 Draw a scatter graph to represent your data.

3 Describe the relationship.

4 Discuss whether you are able to predict a person's height from the size of their feet.

4.2 Time series

- A line graph used to illustrate data collected at regular time intervals (e.g. hourly, daily, weekly, …) is called a **time series** graph.

- **Moving averages** are used to show the trend in time series graphs. They 'even out' seasonal variations in the data.

- To find the n-**point moving averages** you find the average for every n data values, moving forward one data value at a time.

- A **trend line** is a 'line of best fit' drawn through the moving averages plotted on a graph.

Example 3

The table below provides information about the number of job vacancies advertised at Ashwell Job Centre during periods from 2003 to 2005.

Year	March	June	September	December
2003	783	885	845	521
2004	721	820	850	482
2005	650	740	763	470

(a) Plot the information as a time series graph.

(b) Comment on the seasonal variations in the number of job vacancies.

(c) Work out the four-point moving averages for the data.

(d) Draw a trend line and find its equation.

(e) Comment on whether or not there is evidence to suggest that the number of job vacancies in Ashwell fell during the period from early 2003 to late 2005.

> For data recorded four times a year, use four-point moving averages.

(a)

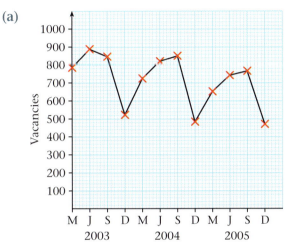

(b) The number of job vacancies falls to a minimum every December, but then climbs again to peak in either June or September.

(c) The four-point moving averages are

$$\frac{783 + 885 + 845 + 521}{4} = 758.5$$

then $\dfrac{885 + 845 + 521 + 721}{4} = 743$

then $\dfrac{845 + 521 + 721 + 820}{4} = 726.75$, etc.

> The first four numbers in the table are: **783**, **885**, **845**, **521**, 721, 820, ...
> The 'next four' numbers are: 783, **885**, **845**, **521**, **721**, 820, ...
> and so on.

The full set of moving averages is as follows

1st	2nd	3rd	4th	5th	6th	7th	8th	9th
758.5	743	726.75	728	718.25	700.5	680.5	658.75	655.75

(d) Four-point moving averages:
y-intercept, $c = 770$
Gradient, $m = \dfrac{110}{-9}$
$= -12.\dot{2}$
Equation $V = -12.2x + 770$
where V is the number of vacancies and x is the number of quarters after Jan 2003.

> Plot each moving average at the mid-point of its time interval. The first moving average is plotted at the mid-point of
> ⊢——┼——⊣
> M J S D
> 2003
> i.e. half way between June and September 2003.

> Draw a trend line that passes through or close to as many points as possible.

(e) The trend line clearly indicates that the number of job vacancies fell between early 2003 and late 2005.

Exercise 4B

1 The numbers of DVDs hired from a shop for each month in 2005 are:

Month	Jan	Feb	Mar	April	May	June	July	Aug	Sept	Oct	Nov	Dec
Number	124	132	125	118	120	98	82	76	110	130	142	128

(a) Plot the information as a time series.
(b) Work out the four-point moving averages and plot these as a graph.
(c) Comment on the variation shown in the data.

2 Jon works as a sales representative. On top of his salary he is paid a bonus according to the number of sales he makes. The bonus is paid three times a year.
The table below provides information about Jon's bonus payments from April 2002 up to December 2005.

Year	April	August	December
2002	£400	£390	£600
2003	£380	£420	£635
2004	£410	£380	£640
2005	£425	£435	£650

(a) Plot this information as a time series.
(b) Work out the three-point moving averages for the data and plot these as a graph.
(c) Draw a trend line for the data.
(d) Find the equation for the trend line.
(e) Comment on your results.

> For data recorded three times a year, use three-point moving averages.

3 The owner of a music shop recorded the number of CDs sold every 3 months.
The table shows his records from January 2004 to June 2005.

Year	Months	Number of CDs
2004	Jan–Mar	270
	Apr–Jun	324
	Jul–Sept	300
	Oct–Dec	258
2005	Jan–Mar	309
	Apr–Jun	335

(a) Calculate the complete set of four-point moving averages for this information.
(b) What trend do these moving averages suggest? [E]

4.3 Retail Price Index

- The **Retail Price Index (RPI)** is calculated each month by the government. It measures the change in price of goods and services.

Example 4

Workwell is a small company.
It is company policy to keep wages in line with changes in the Retail Price Index (RPI).

Sam joined Workwell on 1 January 1987.
His weekly wage then was exactly £100.
For the next 19 years he stayed at Workwell doing the same job.
Work out Sam's weekly wage in

	RPI
Jan 1987	100
Jan 1997	154.4
Jan 2006	193.4

(a) January 1997

(b) January 2006.

(a) In January 1987 the RPI was 100.
In January 1997 the RPI was 154.4.
So the proportional change (or factor) in the RPI

$$= \frac{154.4}{100} = 1.544.$$

So Sam's wage in January 1997 was
wage in January 1987 $\times$ proportional change in RPI
$= £100 \times 1.544 = £154.40$

(b) In January 2006 the RPI was 193.4.
So the proportional change in RPI between January 1987

and January 2001 was $\frac{193.4}{100} = 1.934.$

So Sam's wage in January 2006 was
£100 $\times$ 1.934 = £193.40.

Example 5

The table below provides information about the Retail Price Index in the UK and in Malta from January 1995 to January 2001.

Year	1995	1996	1997	1998	1999	2000	2001
RPI (UK)	146.0	150.2	154.4	159.5	163.4	166.6	171.1
RPI (Malta)	100	99.87	103.57	107.10	108.62	112.24	112.95

(a) On the same axes, draw time series graphs for both sets of RPIs.

(b) Plot the RPI in Malta against the RPI in the UK as points on a scatter graph.

(c) On your scatter graph draw the line of best fit.

(d) Comment on the correlation between the RPI in Malta and the RPI in the UK.

The local newspaper in Malta claimed that price rises on the island between 1995 and 2001 had been lower than price rises in the UK over the same period.

(e) Comment on the newspaper's claim.

(a)

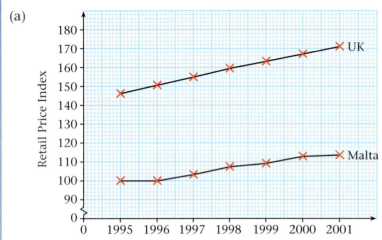

(b) (c)

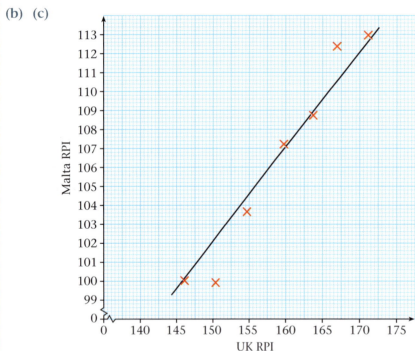

(d) The scatter diagram shows **positive correlation** between the RPI in the UK and the RPI in Malta.

(e) Between 1995 and 2001 the proportional changes in RPI were:

For UK: $\dfrac{171.1}{146.0} = 1.1719$ For Malta: $\dfrac{112.95}{100} = 1.1295$

The change in RPI for the UK is greater than the change in RPI for Malta over the period from 1995 to 2001.
The newspaper's claim is correct.

Exercise 4C

1 Asif joined Wellworkers Ltd in August 1996.
His salary was then £12 500 per year.
The RPI in August 1996 was 153.1.
In August 2005 the RPI was 192.6.
Between August 1996 and August 2005, Asif received salary
increases in line with changes in the RPI.
Work out Asif's salary in August 2005.

2 In January 1975 the RPI was 30.39.
In January 2006 the RPI was 193.4.
In January 1975 the price of a loaf of bread was 12p.
Assuming that bread prices follow the changes in the RPI, work
out the price of a similar loaf of bread in January 2006.

3 In December 2005 the RPI was 194.1.
In December 1960 the RPI was 12.62.
The price of a loaf of bread was 68p in December 2005.
Stating your assumptions, work out an estimate of the price of a
similar loaf of bread in December 1960.

4 The table below provides information about the Retail Price
Index in the UK and on the island of Guernsey during the
months of September from 1994 to 2001.

	1994	1995	1996	1997	1998	1999	2000	2001
UK	145.0	150.6	153.8	159.3	164.4	166.2	171.7	174.6
Guernsey	100.2	104.2	106.2	110.9	115.4	117.4	122.7	125.9

(a) On the same axes draw time series graphs for both sets of RPIs.

(b) Plot the two sets of data as points on a scatter graph.

(c) Draw the line of best fit on the scatter graph.

(d) Comment on the relationship between the RPI in the UK and
the RPI on Guernsey.

A local radio station on Guernsey claims that during the years
from 1994 to 2001 the prices have risen less on the island than in
mainland UK.

(e) Explain whether the table of RPIs provides evidence to
support this claim or not.

Activity – Investigating house prices

1   Collect information from the internet about the average price of
houses in the UK for the years 2000 to the present.

2   Draw suitable graphs and comment on your findings.

Mixed exercise 4

1 The table shows the population of the United Kingdom in each National Census from 1911 to 2001.

Year	1911	1921	1931	1951	1961	1971	1981	1991	2001
Population (millions)	42.1	44.0	46.0	50.2	52.8	55.9	56.4	57.4	59.1

   (a) Find an estimate for the population of the United Kingdom in 1941.

   (b) Plot this information as a time series graph.

   (c) Comment on your results.

2 The table shows information about the depth of tread of seven motorbike tyres and the distance each has travelled.

Distance travelled (1000 km)	8	56	32	14	66	50	38
Depth of tread (mm)	7.1	2.4	4.9	6.6	1.4	3.1	4.1

   (a) Draw a scatter graph to show this information.

   (b) What do you notice about the distance travelled and the depth of tread?

   (c) Draw the line of best fit.

   The depth of tread for another motorbike tyre is 1 mm.

   (d) Find an estimate for the distance travelled by this tyre.

3 The scatter graph shows information about the height, y cm, of a plant, x days after germination. The line of best fit has been drawn on the graph.

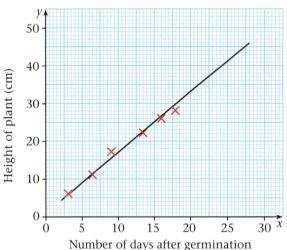

   (a) Use the line of best fit to find an estimate for the height of the plant
       (i) 11 days after germination   **(ii)** 25 days after germination.

   (b) Which of your two answers in **(a)** is likely to be more reliable? Give a reason for your answer.

   (c) Work out the equation of the line of best fit.

4 A glass of water was put in a freezer. The table shows the temperature of the water every 10 minutes.

Time, x minutes	10	20	30	40	50	60
Temperature, y °C	19	16	13	12	11	8

(a) Draw a scatter graph to show this information.

(b) What type of correlation is shown on the scatter graph?

(c) Draw a line of best fit.

(d) Find an estimate for the time when the temperature of the water reaches 0 °C.

(e) Work out the equation of the line of best fit.

5 Fiona breeds cats.
The table shows the numbers of cats born each quarter for the last two years.

Year	2004				2005			
Quarter	1	2	3	4	1	2	3	4
Number of cats	15	29	24	20	19	37	36	22

(a) Draw a time series graph for this information.

(b) Calculate the four-point moving averages and plot them on your graph.

(c) Draw a trend line and comment on the trend in the number of cats born.

6 The table shows the quarterly petrol bills for a company car.

	January	April	July	October
2003	£104.74	£112.15	£97.70	£107.79
2004	£100.50	£114.42	£86.32	£107.38
2005	£121.38	£115.68	£88.23	£101.64

(a) Use the information in the table to draw a graph.

(b) Calculate the four-point moving averages and plot them on your graph.

(c) Comment on your results.

7 The table shows information about the termly absences from school for a class over three years.

	Autumn	Spring	Summer
Year 9	8	43	21
Year 10	11	121	24
Year 11	17	46	36

(a) Draw a time series graph to show this information.

(b) Calculate the values of a suitable moving average and plot them on your graph.

(c) Comment on the trend in the number of absences for this class.

8 In January 1987 the RPI was 100
  In January 2005 the RPI was 188.9
  In January 1987 the price of a packet of crisps was 15p.
  Assuming that the price of a packet of crisps follows the changes
  in the RPI, work out the price of a similar packet of crisps in
  January 2005.

9 In December 1980 the RPI was 69.86
  In December 2000 the RPI was 172.2
  In December 1980 the price of a Christmas tree was £12.50.
  Assuming that the prices of Christmas trees follow the changes in
  the RPI, work out the price of a Christmas tree in December 2000.

Summary of key points

1 A linear relationship between two sets of data is called a
  correlation.

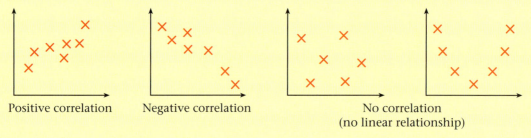

Positive correlation   Negative correlation   No correlation
                                                   (no linear relationship)

2 The **line of best fit** is a straight line that passes through or as close
  to as many of the plotted points as possible.

3 A line of best fit gives a model for how two variables are related. The
  closer the plotted points are to the line, the better the correlation.

4 A line of best fit can be used to estimate other data values within
  the range of the data given.

> You cannot be sure
> that the pattern
> continues outside this
> range.

5 The equation of the line of best fit has the form $y = mx + c$, where
  m is the gradient and c is the intercept with the y-axis.

6 A line graph used to illustrate data collected at regular time
  intervals (e.g. hourly, daily, weekly, …) is called a **time series** graph.

7 **Moving averages** are used to show the trend in time series
  graphs. They 'even out' seasonal variations in the data.

8 To find the **n-point moving averages** you find the average for
  every n data values, moving forward one data value at a time.

9 A **trend line** is a 'line of best fit' drawn through the moving
  averages plotted on a graph.

10 The **Retail Price Index (RPI)** is calculated each month by the
  government. It measures the change in price of goods and services.

5 Probability

- An event which is **certain to happen** has a probability of **1**.
- An event which **cannot happen** has a probability of **0**.
- The probability that an event will happen is always greater than or equal to 0 (impossible) and less than or equal to 1 (certain).

  $0 \leqslant$ probability $\leqslant 1$
- The **theoretical probability** that an event will happen is

  theoretical probability $= \dfrac{\text{number of successful outcomes}}{\text{total number of possible outcomes}}$

  assuming that the outcomes are all equally likely.
- Outcomes are **mutually exclusive** when they cannot happen at the same time.

5.1 Finding probabilities

Example 1

The diagram represents a regular octagonal spinner.
The spinner is to be spun once.
Work out the probability of the spinner stopping on

(a) the letter B   (b) the letter D   (c) a vowel.

(a) The spinner has 8 sections. 1 section is labelled B.

  So $P(B) = \dfrac{\text{number of successful outcomes}}{\text{total number of possible outcomes}} = \dfrac{1}{8}$

| The 8 outcomes are all equally likely. |

(b) $P(D) = \frac{2}{8}$

(c) Of the letters A, B, C, D and E the vowels are A and E.
  A and E occupy a total of 4 sections out of 8.

  So $P(\text{vowel}) = \frac{4}{8} = \frac{1}{2}$

| You cannot spin an A **and** an E on the spinner at *the same time*. These are mutually exclusive events. |

- The **estimated probability** that an event will happen in a game or experiment is

  estimated probability $= \dfrac{\text{number of successful trials}}{\text{total number of trials}}$
- The **estimated probability** is given by the **relative frequency** with which an event occurs in a trial or experiment.
- The **relative frequency** of an outcome in an experiment is

  relative probability $= \dfrac{\text{number of successful trials}}{\text{total number of trials}}$

  This is also called the experimental probability.

Example 2

There are four candidates in an election:

Patel, Roberts, Smith, Taylor

Before the election a market research company asked a random sample of 1200 people which person they intended to vote for in the election. The response to the survey was as follows:

Patel	Roberts	Smith	Taylor
317	452	203	228

In the actual election 24 850 votes will be cast.

Work out, with a reason, an estimate of the likely number of votes that will be cast for Roberts.

The estimated probability that a vote cast is for Roberts $= \frac{452}{1200} = 0.376\,666$.

So an estimate for P(R) = 0.376 666.

For the election, $P(R) = 0.376\,666 = \dfrac{\text{no. of votes cast for Roberts}}{24\,850}$

So the likely number of votes cast for Roberts = 24 850 × 0.376 666
= 9360.1666
= 9360 (to the nearest whole number).

The turnout for the 2005 General Election in the UK was 61.4%.

You cannot have a fraction of a vote.

Example 3

The diagram represents a biased spinner.

Tom spun the spinner 200 times.
His results were

Section	A	B	C	D	E
Frequency	45	27	64	34	30

Asha then spun the same spinner 300 times.
Her results were

Section	A	B	C	D	E
Frequency	69	38	98	50	45

(a) Work out the best estimate of the probability of the spinner stopping on section C when it is spun once.

Kenneth spun the spinner 1200 times.
He did not record the results.

(b) Work out the best estimate for the number of times the spinner stopped on section E during the 1200 spins.

(a) For the best estimate pool Tom's and Asha's results.
   In 200 + 300 = 500 spins, there were 64 + 98 = 162 Cs.

$$\text{Estimated probability } P(C) = \frac{\text{number of successful trials}}{\text{total number of trials}}$$

$$= \frac{162}{500} = 0.324$$

(b) Estimated probability $P(E) = \dfrac{30 + 45}{500} = \dfrac{75}{500} = 0.15$

For 1200 spins

$$P(E) = \frac{\text{number of times spinner stops on E}}{1200}$$

So estimate for number of times spinner
stops on E = 1200 × P(E)
= 1200 × 0.15
= 180

> The greater the number of trials, the better the estimate of the probability.

> Each 'spin' is a 'trial'. The successful trials are the 'C's.

> Pooling Tom and Asha's results.

Exercise 5A

1 A bag contains 20 equal-sized number cards.
   • Five are numbered 2
   • Two are numbered 3
   • Three are numbered 4
   • Six are numbered 5
   • The remainder are numbered 6.
   A number card is selected at random.
   Work out the probability that the selected card will have

   (a) the number 6   **(b)** an even number

   (c) a prime number   **(d)** a multiple of 3.

2 A train is defined as 'late' if it arrives at the station 3 or more
   minutes after its scheduled arrival time.
   Explain how you could work out an estimate for the probability
   of a train being late.

3 Jane is conducting a survey into the number of goals scored in
   first-class football matches. She has data on 200 matches, as
   shown below.

Number of goals	0	1	2	3	4	5	6	7
Number of matches	7	23	36	96	22	9	6	1

   (a) Work out, with a reason, an estimate for the probability of a
   first-class football match finishing with
      (i) exactly four goals being scored
      (ii) four or more goals being scored.
   During a season, 5200 first-class football matches are played.
   (b) Work out an estimate for the most likely number of games in
   which exactly three goals will be scored.

4   The diagram represents a biased pentagonal spinner with sections
    labelled A, B, C, D and E.
    When the spinner is spun once, the probabilities of it stopping
    on each of the letters are given in the table below.

Letter	A	B	C	D	E
Probability	0.23	0.18	0.15	0.25	0.19

The spinner is to be spun 600 times.
Work out an estimate for the likely number of times it will stop
on B.

5   The diagram shows a four-sided spinner.
    It is thought that the spinner is biased.
    Carla spins the spinner 100 times and records the letter it stops on.
    Here are her results.

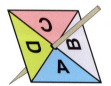

Letter	A	B	C	D
Frequency	33	27	20	20

Miles then spins the spinner 100 times and records the letter it
stops on.
Here are his results.

Letter	A	B	C	D
Frequency	30	28	19	23

(a) Explain why there is a difference between the two sets of
     results.

(b) Use the information to calculate the *best* estimate for the
     probability that the spinner will land on each of the four letters.

(c) Explain whether or not the spinner appears to be biased.

> To see if the spinner
> is fair, compare its
> experimental results
> with the theoretical
> probability.

Activity – Estimating probability on a spinner

Design and make your own spinner. Label one section **A**.

Spin the spinner 10, 20, 30, …, 100 times and count the number of times it lands on **A**.

Copy and complete the table.

Number of spins	Number of times it lands on A	Estimated probability
10		
20		
…		
…		
100		

Draw a graph to show Estimated probability (on the vertical axis) against Number of spins (on the
horizontal axis).

Comment on your results.

5.2 **Listing outcomes**

Example 4

This square-shaped spinner is spun once.
A coin is thrown once.
One possible joint outcome of the two events is
    (1, Head)

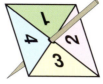

(a) List all possible joint outcomes of the two events.

(b) Explain why the probability of the spinner landing on 1 and
     the coin landing Head is $\frac{1}{8}$.

(a) (1, Head)   (1, Tail)
     (2, Head)   (2, Tail)
     (3, Head)   (3, Tail)
     (4, Head)   (4, Tail)

> List the outcomes
> systematically.

(b) There are 8 possible outcomes.
     Each of these outcomes is equally likely. There is one
     successful outcome (1, Head).
     P(1, Head) = $\frac{1}{8}$.

- A **sample space diagram** represents all possible outcomes of one or
  more events.

Example 5

The diagram represents a fair coin and a fair spinner.
The spinner is in the shape of an equilateral triangle.
Asif throws the coin once and spins the spinner once.

 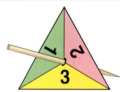

(a) Construct a sample space diagram to show all the
     possible joint outcomes.

(b) Work out the probability of the joint outcome Head and a number less than 3.

(a)
```
3      ●    ●
     (H, 3) (T, 3)

2      ●    ●
     (H, 2) (T, 2)

1      ●    ●
     (H, 1) (T, 1)

       H    T
```

(b) For the joint outcome Head and a number less than 3, the 'successful' outcomes are
         (H, 1) (H, 2)
     There are 6 joint outcomes in total.

> You do not have to simplify the fraction
> unless the question asks you to.

     P(H and number < 3) = $\frac{2}{6}$ (or $\frac{1}{3}$)

Exercise 5B

1 Tamsin has four places to visit:
  London, Manchester, Bristol and Edinburgh.
  In each case she has three possible methods of travelling:
  car, bus or train.
  One possible journey she could make is
  London by train.
  List all the possible journeys Tamsin could make.

2 This spinner is spun once and the dice is rolled once.
  One possible joint outcome is (A, 1).
  (a) Draw a sample space diagram to show all the
    possible joint outcomes.
  (b) Write down the probability of the joint outcome (A, 1).
  (c) Write down the probability of the joint outcome (D, 3).

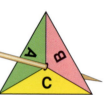

3 A game is played with two fair spinners. The spinners are spun at
  the same time.
  The diagram below shows the result (Red, 3).

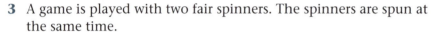
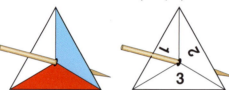

  (a) Draw a sample space diagram to show all the possible results
    when the spinners are spun once.
  (b) Work out the probability of (Blue, 1) when the spinners are
    spun once.

4 Kylie has a fair coin and a fair six-sided dice.
  She throws the coin once.
  She rolls the dice once.
  The diagram shows the outcome (Head, 3).
  (a) Draw a sample space diagram to show all the
    possible outcomes.
  (b) Work out the probability of the result (Tail, 6).

5.3 Independent events and tree diagrams

⊙ 24 Probability trees

- Two events are **independent** if the outcome of one event does not
  affect the outcome of the other event.
- The sum of the probabilities of all mutually exclusive outcomes = 1.
- If the probability that an event occurs is p than the probability that it
  does *not* occur is $1 - p$.

Example 6

The probability of a newly laid egg being cracked is 0.008.
(a) Work out the probability of a newly laid egg *not* being cracked.

A supermarket orders 120 000 newly laid eggs.
(b) Work out the best estimate for the number of these eggs which are likely to be cracked.

(a) P(not cracked) = 1 − P(cracked)
$$= 1 - 0.008$$
$$= 0.992$$

(b) For the batch of 120 000 eggs

$$P(\text{cracked}) = 0.008 = \frac{\text{estimated number cracked}}{120\,000}$$

So estimated number cracked = 0.008 × 120 000
$$= 960$$

- For mutually exclusive events, the probability that A occurs **or** B occurs is **P(A) + P(B)**.
- For independent events, the probability that A occurs **and** B occurs is **P(A) × P(B)**.

Example 7

The school bus can be either *late* or *not late*.
On any day, the probability of the school bus being *late* = 0.15.

(a) Complete the probability tree diagram for the school bus on Monday and Tuesday.

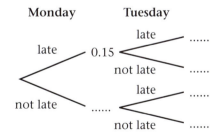

(b) Work out
    (i) the probability of the school bus being late on both Monday and Tuesday
    (ii) the probability of the school bus being late on at least one of these two days
    (iii) the probability of the school bus being late on at least one day during the five days of a school week.

(a)

	Monday	Tuesday	

The events 'late on Monday' and 'late on Tuesday' are independent events. So the probabilities are both 0.15.

late — 0.15 — late — 0.15
     not late — 0.85

not late — 0.85 — late — 0.15
     not late — 0.85

P(not late) = 1 − P(late)

(b) (i) The probability of the school bus being late on Monday and late on Tuesday is

$$0.15 \times 0.15 = 0.0225$$

For independent events the probability that A occurs *and* B occurs is P(A) × P(B).

(ii) From the tree diagram, the possible joint outcomes are

Mon	Tues
late	late •
late	not late •
not late	late •
not late	not late

For these three outcomes the bus is late on at least one day.

Method 1
Work out the probability of each of the three joint outcomes and add them together.

    late, late   late, not late   not late, late
$(0.15 \times 0.15) + (0.15 \times 0.85) + (0.85 \times 0.15)$
=   0.0225   +   0.1275   +   0.1275
=   0.2775

The three outcomes are mutually exclusive, so P(A or B or C) = P(A) + P(B) + P(C).

Method 2
Work out the probability of the bus *not* being late on either day, and subtract from 1.
P(not late, not late) = 0.85 × 0.85
                = 0.7225
P(late at least once) = 1 − P(not late, not late)
                  = 1 − 0.7225
                  = 0.2775

The bus being late on *at least* one day means it is late on one or two days.

(iii) Probability of the bus being late on at least one day of the week = 1 − probability of it not being late on all five days.

Probability (not late on all five days) =
$0.85 \times 0.85 \times 0.85 \times 0.85 \times 0.85 = 0.85^5$
                                     = 0.4437 (to 4 d.p.)
So probability of bus being late on at least one day of the week = 1 − 0.4437
                    = 0.5563 (4 d.p.)

Exercise 5C

1 An airline checks the departure times of 200 flights.
Of the 200 flights, 12 take off early, 142 take off on time and the remainder are late.

   (a) Work out the best estimate of the probability that a randomly selected flight departs late.

   (b) There are 720 flights in one month. Work out the best estimate for the number of these flights that are likely to depart late.

2 The probability that Sharon will pass her Science examination is 0.7.
The probability that she will pass her Music examination is 0.9.
Given that passing Music and passing Science are independent, work out the probability

   (a) of Sharon passing both examinations

   (b) of Sharon passing Science and failing Music

   (c) of Sharon passing at least one of these examinations.

3 Casey and Nicole are both due to take their driving test.
The probability that Casey will pass is 0.8.
The probability that Nicole will pass is 0.6.

   (a) Work out the probability that they both pass the driving test.

   (b) Work out the probability that at least one of them passes the driving test.

4 A biased dice has faces labelled 1, 2, 3, 4, 5 and 6.
When it is rolled once, the probabilities of each score are:

Score	1	2	3	4	5	6
Probability	0.18	0.13	0.21	0.17	0.16	

   (a) Work out the probability of a score of 6 when the dice is rolled once.

The dice is to be rolled twice.

   (b) Work out the probability
      (i) of two 1s
     (ii) of the same score twice
    (iii) that the sum of the scores is 4.

5 The England and Australia cricket teams toss an ordinary coin at the start of each of the five test matches.

   (a) Work out the probability that Australia will win the toss on all five occasions.

   (b) Work out the probability of England winning the toss at least once.

6 A train leaves the station either *on time* or *late*.

   (a) Copy and complete the probability tree diagram.

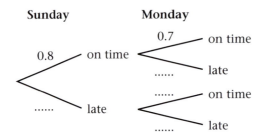

    Sunday   **Monday**

   (b) Work out the probability of the train being late on both days.

   (c) Work out the probability of the train being late at least once out of the two days.

Mixed exercise 5

1 The diagram represents a biased spinner.

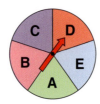

Melachi spins the spinner 100 times and records the letter it stops on each time.
His results are

Letter	A	B	C	D	E
Frequency	17	26	31	9	17

Tilly spins the spinner 200 times and records the letter it stops on each time.
Her results are

Letter	A	B	C	D	E
Frequency	39	48	69	21	23

   (a) Tilly spun the spinner twice as many times as Malachi.
   Explain why the frequencies in Tilly's table of results are not double those in Malachi's table.

   (b) Work out the best estimate of the probability of the spinner stopping on

       (i) B   **(ii)** D   **(iii)** a vowel

   when it is spun once.

2 The diagram represents a biased spinner. When it is spun once the probabilities of it stopping on each section are

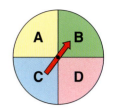

Section	A	B	C	D
Probability	0.32	0.22	0.17	0.29

The spinner is spun 1200 times.
Work out an estimate for the likely number of times it stops on section C.

3 The diagram represents a spinner.
The spinner was spun 10 000 times and the sections it stopped on were recorded. The results are

Section	A	B	C	D	E
No. of times	593	4009	1427	2003	1968

Explain clearly whether or not this information suggests that the spinner is biased.

4 A bag contains five equal-sized beads. Three of these beads are blue and two of them are red. A second bag contains eight equal-sized beads. Three of these beads are blue and five of them are red.
Ayesha selects, at random, one bead from each bag.
Work out the probability that

(a) both beads are blue

(b) both beads are the same colour

(c) the beads are different colours.

5 Chelsea has ten mugs. Six of the mugs are red and four are blue.
In the morning she picks one mug at random from the ten mugs.
In the afternoon she also picks one mug from the same ten mugs.

(a) Copy and complete the probability tree diagram.

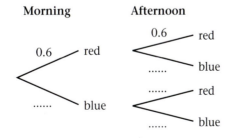

(b) Work out the probability that Chelsea will pick a red mug both in the morning and in the afternoon.

(c) Work out the probability that Chelsea will pick one mug of each colour.

6   There are three red marbles and two blue marbles in a bag.
    Sophie takes a marble at random from the bag and replaces it.
    She then takes another marble at random from the bag.
    Find the probability that both the marbles she takes are the same
    colour.

7   Mark spins a biased coin 40 times. It comes down Heads 31 times.
    Calculate an estimate for the number of times he would expect
    the coin to come down Heads if he spins it 600 times.

8   When Sarah and Louise play a game of tennis, the probability
    that Sarah will win is 0.3.
    When they play a game of snooker, the probability that Sarah
    will win is 0.2.
    Neither game can ever end in a tie.
    Sarah and Louise play a game of tennis and then a game of snooker.

    (a) Copy and complete the probability tree diagram for winning
        the games.

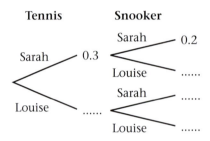

    (b) Work out the probability that
        (i) Sarah wins both games
        (ii) Louise wins at least one of the games.
    Next year the girls will play tennis against each other 80 times.
    (c) Work out the best estimate for the likely number of these
        games that Sarah will win.

9   The probability of a new battery being faulty is 0.03.
    (a) Work out the probability of a new battery not being faulty.
    A large chain of shops orders 600 000 of these new batteries.
    (b) Work out an estimate for the most likely number of these
        600 000 batteries that will be faulty.
    Aziz buys a pack of three of these batteries.
    (c) Work out the probability of all three of these batteries being
        faulty.
        Give your reasoning.

10 The probability of a new computer chip being faulty is 0.0003.
    (a) Work out the probability of a new chip not being faulty.
    A company produces 12 million of these chips.
    (b) Work out an estimate of the most likely number of these
        chips to be faulty.

11 When Jim and Andy play a computer game, the probability of Jim winning is 0.8.
When they play a game of squash, the probability of Jim winning is 0.3.
Tomorrow they are due to play a computer game and a game of squash.

   (a) Work out the probability of Jim losing both games.

   (b) Work out the probability of Andy winning at least one game.

12 Tom has two bags of letter tiles.
Tiles with the letters A, B and C are in one bag and tiles with the letters D, E, F and G are in the other bag.
He picks a tile at random from each bag.

   (a) Show the combined outcomes in a tree diagram.

   (b) List the combined outcomes.

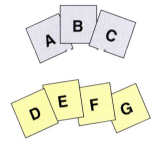

Summary of key points

1 An event which is **certain to happen** has a probability of **1**.

2 An event which **cannot happen** has a probability of **0**.

3 The probability that an event will happen is always greater than or equal to 0 (impossible) and less than or equal to 1 (certain).

$$0 \leqslant \text{probability} \leqslant 1$$

4 The **theoretical probability** that an event will happen is

$$\text{theoretical probability} = \frac{\text{number of successful outcomes}}{\text{total number of possible outcomes}}$$

assuming that the outcomes are all equally likely.

5 Outcomes are **mutually exclusive** when they cannot happen at the same time.

6 The **estimated probability** that an event will happen in a game or experiment is

$$\text{estimated probability} = \frac{\text{number of successful trials}}{\text{total number of trials}}$$

7 The **estimated probability** is given by the **relative frequency** with which an event occurs in a trial or experiment.

8 The **relative frequency** of an outcome in an experiment is

$$\text{relative probability} = \frac{\text{number of successful trials}}{\text{total number of trials}}$$

This is also called the experimental probability.

9 A **sample space diagram** represents all possible outcomes of one or more events.

10 Two events are **independent** if the outcome of one event does not affect the outcome of the other event.

11 The sum of the probabilities of all mutually exclusive outcomes $= 1$.

12 If the probability that an event occurs is p than the probability that it does *not* occur is $1 - p$.

13 For mutually exclusive events, the probability that A occurs **or** B occurs is **P(A) + P(B)**.

14 For independent events, the probability that A occurs **and** B occurs is **P(A) × P(B)**.

6 More probability

6.1 Conditional probability

29 Drawing probability trees

- **Conditional probability** is when the probability of an event is dependent on the probability of a previous event. Think of the probability depending on the 'conditions' before the event.

When events are not independent their probabilities are conditional.

Example 1

A box contains nine discs. Four of the discs are yellow and five are blue.
Two discs are removed at random from the box.
Calculate the probability that

(a) both discs will be yellow

(b) only one of the discs will be yellow.

Draw a tree diagram to show the probabilities.

The probability of blue or yellow in the second choice is conditional upon the colour picked in the first choice.

First choice — **Second choice**

yellow $\frac{4}{9}$ → yellow $\frac{3}{8}$, blue $\frac{5}{8}$

blue $\frac{5}{9}$ → yellow $\frac{4}{8}$, blue $\frac{4}{8}$

If a yellow disc is picked first and not replaced there will be only eight discs left to choose from. Three of these will be yellow. So the probability of choosing a yellow disc is $\frac{3}{8}$.

(a) The probability that both discs will be yellow is
$$\frac{4}{9} \times \frac{3}{8} = \frac{12}{72}$$

(b) The probability that only one disc will be yellow is
P(yellow, blue) + P(blue, yellow)
$$= (\frac{4}{9} \times \frac{3}{8}) + (\frac{5}{9} \times \frac{4}{8}) = \frac{12}{72} + \frac{20}{72} = \frac{32}{72}$$

If a blue disc is picked first and not replaced there will be eight discs left to choose from. Four of these will be yellow. So the probability of choosing a yellow disc is $\frac{4}{8}$.

Any exactly correct equivalent fraction would gain full marks. Answers such as 0.4, 0.44 or 44% are not sufficiently accurate. The answer must be exact, for example $\frac{4}{9}$ or $0.\dot{4}$.

• Cut down the work by only drawing paths through the tree diagram that you need to solve the problem. But make sure you include *all* the paths you need.

Example 2

There are eight HB pencils and five H pencils in a tin.
Three pencils are removed one at a time from the tin.
Work out the probability that all three pencils will be HB pencils.

To select three HB pencils you need to select an HB each time.
The path for this in the tree diagram is

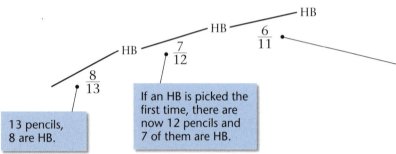

If HBs were picked the first and second times, there are now 11 pencils and 6 of them are HB.

If an HB is picked the first time, there are now 12 pencils and 7 of them are HB.

13 pencils, 8 are HB.

So the probability that all three pencils picked are HB is

$$\frac{8}{13} \times \frac{7}{12} \times \frac{6}{11} = \frac{336}{1716}$$

Example 3

Mrs Taylor calculates that if a student does their homework regularly than the probability that they will pass the examination is 0.85; but if the student does not do their homework regularly than the probability that they will pass the examination is only 0.6.
Given that only 75% of her students do their homework regularly, calculate the probability that a student selected at random will pass the examination.

Show the probabilities in a tree diagram.

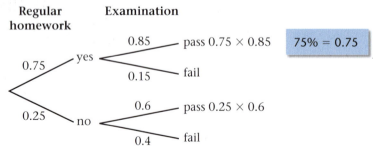

75% = 0.75

So, the probability that a student selected at random will pass the examination is

$$(0.75 \times 0.85) + (0.25 \times 0.6) = 0.7875.$$

Exercise 6A

1 A bag contains seven green balls and three blue balls. A ball is removed at random from the bag and it is not replaced. A second ball is removed. Copy and complete the tree diagram.

Sampling 'without replacement' always involves conditional probability.

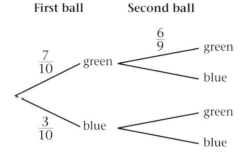

      First ball   **Second ball**

(a) Work out the probability that the balls will both be green.

(b) Work out the probability that only one of the balls will be green.

2 A bag contains nine red balls and six white balls. A ball is removed at random from the bag and it is not replaced. A second ball is removed.

(a) Draw a tree diagram to show the probabilities.

(b) Work out the probability that the balls will
    (i) both be white
   (ii) both be the same colour
  (iii) be different colours.

3 There are 20 sweets in a bag. Eight of them are strawberry flavour. Three sweets are removed from the bag, one at a time. None of the sweets are replaced.
Calculate the probability that all three sweets are strawberry flavour.

4 The performance of a racing car is affected by the weather.
In dry weather the racing car skids with a probability of $\frac{1}{3}$, but in wet weather the racing car skids with a probability of $\frac{4}{5}$.
In the racing season the probability it will rain on any day is $\frac{1}{8}$.
The racing car is entered for a race during the racing season.
Calculate the probability that the car will skid in the race.

5 Group A has three men and five women.
Group B has four men and six women.
A fair dice is rolled. If the number on the dice is 5 or more then a person is picked at random from group A, otherwise a person is picked at random from group B.
Find the probability that the person selected will be a man.

Mixed exercise 6

1 A bag contains three red balls, two yellow balls and five green balls.
   A ball is taken at random and not replaced.
   A second ball is then taken from the bag.

   (a) Copy and complete the tree diagram below.

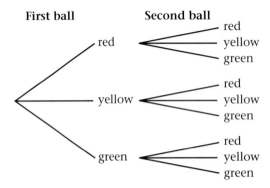

First ball   **Second ball**
            red   red
                        yellow
                        green
            yellow   red
                        yellow
                        green
            green   red
                        yellow
                        green

   (b) Use the tree diagram to calculate the probability that
        (i) both balls will be red
        (ii) both balls will be the same colour
        (iii) exactly one of the balls will be red.

2 To start a game Harold must throw a 6 with a dice.
   For a fair dice, calculate the probability that Harold starts the
   game on his

   (a) first throw   (b) second throw   (c) fifth throw.

3 Box A contains four red discs and three white discs.
   Box B contains five red discs and two white discs.
   A disc is taken at random from box A and put into box B.
   A disc is now taken at random from box B.
   Calculate the probability that this disc will be (a) red (b) white.

4 The letters of the word PARALLELOGRAM are written on tiles and
   placed in a bag. Two tiles are selected at random.
   Calculate the probability that both letters will be an L.

5 Box X contains seven yellow discs and three black discs.
   Box Y contains six yellow discs and four black discs.
   Box Z contains five yellow discs and five black discs.
   A fair dice is thrown.
   If the number on the dice is a 1 or a 2, a disc is taken at random
   from box X.
   If the number on the dice is a 3, 4 or 5, a disc is taken at random
   from box Y.
   If the number on the dice is a 6, a disc is taken at random from
   box Z.
   Calculate the probability that the disc will be (a) yellow (b) black.

6   Two different students are chosen at random from nine boys and seven girls.
    Calculate the probability that the students chosen will be

    (a) the two youngest students   (b) both girls.

7   A golfer observes that she hits a straight drive at a hole on 75% of the occasions when the weather is not windy, but on only 45% of the occasions when the weather is windy.
    Weather records in the region show that it is windy on 35% of all days.
    Calculate the probability that on any randomly selected day, the golfer will hit a straight drive at the hole.

8   In a class of 25 girls, nine have blond hair.

    (a) If two girls are selected at random from the class, calculate the probability that
            (i)   they will both have blond hair
            (ii) neither of them will have blond hair.

    (b) If three girls are selected at random, find the probability that more than one of them will have blond hair.

Summary of key points

- **Conditional probability** is when the probability of an event is dependent on the probability of a previous event. Think of the probability depending on the 'conditions' before the event.

- Cut down the work by only drawing paths through the tree diagram that you need to solve the problem. But make sure you include *all* the paths you need.

> When events are not independent their probabilities are conditional.

Examination practice paper

Section A (calculator)

1   A bag contains yellow, red and blue balls.
    Carl takes one ball at random from the bag.
    The table shows the probabilities that Carl will take a yellow ball
    or a red ball.

Colour	Yellow	Red	Blue
Probability	0.25	0.3	

   (a) Work out the probability that Carl takes a yellow ball
        or a red ball.   **(2 marks)**
   (b) Work out the probability that Carl takes a blue ball.
                                                                   (2 marks)

2   Matt recorded the number of letters delivered to his house in April.
    Here are his results.

Number of letters	Frequency	
0	3	
1	7	
2	8	
3	8	
4	4	

    Work out the mean number of letters delivered to his
    house per day.   **(3 marks)**

3   This stem and leaf diagram shows the times, in minutes,
    for each of 19 students to complete their English homework.

    Time to complete homework (minutes)
    1 | 2, 9
    2 | 0, 1, 1, 3, 5, 6, 8, 9
    3 | 3, 5, 5, 7, 7, 8, 8
    4 | 1, 5   Key: 4|1 means 41

    On a copy of the grid, draw a box plot to represent this
    information.

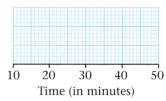

                                                                   (4 marks)

4 Luggage is weighed before it is put on an aeroplane.
The total weight, in kg, of the luggage for each family
travelling on an aeroplane is recorded.
Some of this information is shown in the table and in
the histogram.

Weight, w (kg)	Frequency	
$10 \leqslant w < 25$	3	
$25 \leqslant w < 35$		
$35 \leqslant w < 40$		
$40 \leqslant w < 45$	10	
$45 \leqslant w < 55$	14	
$55 \leqslant w < 70$	8	

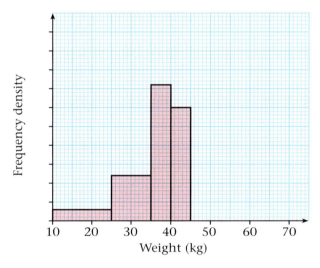

(a) Copy the frequency table. Use the information given
to complete it. **(2 marks)**

(b) Copy the histogram. Use the information given to
complete it. **(2 marks)**

Total for Section A: 15 marks

Section B (non-calculator)

1 The scatter graph shows information about the height and arm span for nine students.

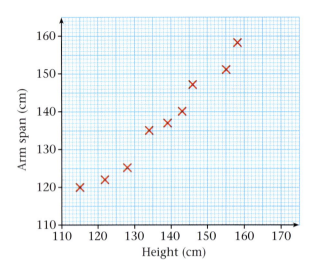

Another student has a height of 130 cm and an arm span of 134 cm.

(a) Plot this information on a copy of the scatter graph. **(1 mark)**

(b) What type of correlation does this scatter graph show? **(1 mark)**

(c) Draw a line of best fit on the scatter graph. **(1 mark)**

The height of another student is 150 cm.

(d) Use your line of best fit to find an estimate for the arm span of this student. **(1 mark)**

2 Carlos does a survey on the amount of time his friends spend watching TV.
He uses this question on a questionnaire.

'How much time do you spend watching TV?'

☐ 1 hour   ☐ 2 hours   ☐ 3 hours

Write down **two** things that are wrong with this question. **(2 marks)**

3 The table shows information about the lifetime, *t* hours, for each of 50 batteries.

Lifetime, *t* (hours)	Frequency
$0 \leqslant t < 5$	4
$5 \leqslant t < 10$	7
$10 \leqslant t < 15$	10
$15 \leqslant t < 20$	12
$20 \leqslant t < 25$	14
$25 \leqslant t < 30$	3

(a) Find the class interval in which the median lies. **(1 mark)**

The cumulative frequency graph for this information has been drawn on the grid.

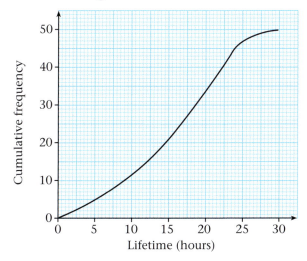

(b) Use this graph to work out an estimate for the interquartile range of the lifetime of the batteries. **(2 marks)**

(c) Use this graph to work out an estimate for the number of batteries with a lifetime of more than 23 hours. **(2 marks)**

4 There are ten discs in a bag.

Three of the discs are blue and seven of the discs are red.

Two discs are taken at random from the bag.

Calculate the probability that only one of the two discs will be red. **(4 marks)**

Total for Section B: 15 marks

Answers

Exercise 1A

1 Give different meal options that are served in the canteen. Ask for the frequency that the different meal options are chosen. Give several different options that students may want to have served in the canteen that are not already served.

2 (a) He needs to specify a time period, e.g. last week or last month; the response options are too vague.
   (b) How many pizzas have you eaten in the last month?
        0   1   2   3   4   5   more than 5

3

Drinks	Tally	Frequency
Coffee	ЖЖ ЖЖ	10
Cola	ЖЖ ||	7
Lemon	||||	4
Tea	ЖЖ ||	7
Orange	|||	3
Milk			1
	TOTAL	32

4

Party	Tally	Frequency
Conservative		
Green		
Labour		
Liberal		
SNP		
Plaid Cymru		

5

Time t (seconds)	Tally	Frequency
$0 < t \leqslant 5$		0
$5 < t \leqslant 10$	||||	4
$10 < t \leqslant 15$	ЖЖ ||	7
$15 < t \leqslant 20$	|||| ЖЖ		11
$20 < t \leqslant 25$	ЖЖ		6
$25 < t \leqslant 30$	ЖЖ ||	7
$30 < t \leqslant 35$	|||	3
$35 < t \leqslant 40$	|||	3
$40 < t \leqslant 45$	ЖЖ |||	8
$45 < t \leqslant 50$		0
$50 < t \leqslant 55$	||||	4
$55 < t \leqslant 60$	||	2
$60 < t \leqslant 65$	||	2
$65 < t \leqslant 70$	||	2
$70 < t \leqslant 75$			1
	TOTAL	60

6

	Videos	DVDs	Totals
Boys	21	17	38
Girls	15	27	42
Totals	36	44	80

7

Age (years)	Male	Female	Total
21–30	1	2	3
31–40	3	7	10
41–50	11	1	12
51–60	7	3	10
Total	22	13	35

8 (a) Internet or catalogues (secondary) or look at prices in shops (primary)
   (b) Questionnaire (primary)
   (c) Ask the headteacher (primary)
   (d) Questionnaire (primary)
   (e) Internet (secondary)

Exercise 1B

1 A
2 B
3 A
4 (a) The manager wants to serve food that all people in the factory will want to buy.
   (b) All people in the factory.
5 It would take too long to find and question them all.

Exercise 1C

1 (a) Number a list of patients from 1 to 1200. Use a calculator to find Ran # × 1200, and then round. Select the patient with this number from the list. repeat until 30 patients have been selected.
   (b) Number a list of patients from 1 to 1200. Use a calculator to find Ran # × 25, and then round. Then, starting with the patient with this number, go through the list and select every 25th patient. For example, if the random number was 3, take the 3rd, 28th, 53rd, ..., all the way to the 1178th patient.
2 (a) 8 caravans
   (b) 12 caravans.
3 (a) (b) Students' own answers
4 Firstly, number the adverts on each page. Use a calculator to find Ran # × 250, and then round. Turn to the page with this number. Use a calculator to find Ran # × 50, and then round. Select the advert with this number on the relevant page. Repeat the whole process until 80 adverts have been selected.
5 (a) 5 boys in Year 10.
   (b) 41 Key Stage 3 students.
6 Use a calculator to find Ran # × 50, and round. Take the name which is this number from the start of the list, and then select every 50th name from the telephone directory.
   For example, if the random number was 37, take the 37th, 87th, 137th, ... etc., name from the telephone directory.

Mixed exercise 1

1 For example:
   (a) The times are too vague.
   (b) How many hours do you listen to the radio each day?
        0–1, 2–3, 4–5, 6–7, 8–9, 10 or more

2 (a)

Age (years)	Male	Female	Total
18 and under	21	**30**	**51**
19–25	**23**	9	32
26 and over	10	7	**17**
Total	54	**46**	100

(b) (i) 51%   **(ii)** 9%

3

	Jazz	Rock	Classical	Folk	Total
Men	12	**17**	19	4	52
Women	9	23	9	7	**48**
Total	21	**40**	28	11	100

4 (a) The question omits many possible methods of communication and cannot be answered by the Yes/No tick boxes.
(b) The number of email addresses is not relevant to how teenagers communicate with each other.

5 The question should specify a time period, e.g. each week. The options are too specific. They would be better as:
less than £1, £1 to £1.99, £2 to £2.99, £3 to £3.99, £4 or more

6 Number a list of students from 1 to 800.
Generate a random number between 1 and 10. Starting with the student with this number select every 10th student from the list.

7

Age (years)	Disco	Barbecue	Garden party
$a < 10$			
$10 \leq a < 15$			
⋮			
$65 \leq a < 70$			

8 (a) For example, use calculator to pick random page, column on a page, line in a column then word in line. Repeat until 20 words are selected.
(b) Make decisions beforehand about: whether or not to include words in quotations; whether or not to include article titles, picture captions, etc.; what to do about pages where text is arranged randomly (do you ignore the page ?).

9 (a) Student's method
(b) The larger the sample, the more accurate the survey. A larger sample takes longer to collect and process.

10 (a)

Age (years)	Number in sample
16	12
17	27
18	21

(b) 515 female students

Exercise 2A

1

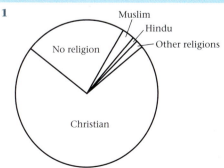

2 Japan 68.75 million, China 53.9 million, Germany 39.6 million, UK 35.75 million

3

```
 9 | 9
10 | 9
11 | 0, 0, 0, 1, 5, 8
12 | 0, 0, 5, 5, 5, 7, 7
13 | 2, 4
14 | 1, 9
15 | 9
16 | 3, 9
17 | 0
18 | 0       Key: 10|9 means 109
```

4

```
 4 | 3, 3, 8, 9
 5 | 1, 3, 7, 8
 6 | 0, 2, 4, 8, 8, 8, 9
 7 | 0, 2, 5, 7
 8 | 1, 1, 2, 4
 9 | 1, 2, 8
10 | 1, 2
11 | 3, 7
```

Exercise 2B

1 (a)

Temp (°C)	Tally	Frequency
$40 \leq t < 50$	卌 I	6
$50 \leq t < 60$	卌 IIII	9
$60 \leq t < 70$	卌 卌 卌 II	17
$70 \leq t < 80$	卌 卌 卌 卌	20
$80 \leq t < 90$	卌 III	8

(b)

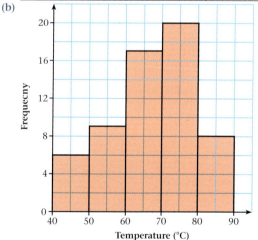

2

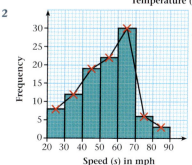

3

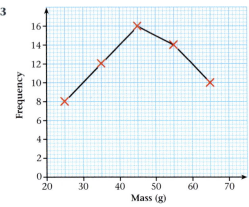

4 (a) There are more young trees and fewer old trees in Hundred Acre Wood than in Wild Wood.
(b) There are 94 trees in Hundred Acre Wood and only 65 trees in Wild Wood.

Exercise 2C

1 (a), (b), (c)

Age (*a*) years	Frequency density for (a), (b) and (c)		
$0 < a \leqslant 20$	0.7	3.5	7
$20 < a \leqslant 30$	2.2	11	22
$30 < a \leqslant 40$	2.5	12.5	25
$40 < a \leqslant 45$	4.8	24	48
$45 < a \leqslant 50$	3.6	18	36
$50 < a \leqslant 60$	3.2	16	32
$60 < a \leqslant 70$	2.6	13	26
$70 < a \leqslant 85$	1	5	10

Class widths   Standard class interval of 5 years   Standard class interval of 10 years

2

Temperature, *t* (°C)	Frequency density
$0 \leqslant t < 30$	0.4
$30 \leqslant t \leqslant 60$	1.97
$60 < t \leqslant 70$	3
$65 < t \leqslant 95$	0.5

(Class widths used to calculate the frequency density)

3

Age, *a* (years)	Frequency density
$0 < a \leqslant 20$	2.75
$20 < a \leqslant 30$	8
$30 < a \leqslant 50$	5
$50 < a \leqslant 60$	7.2
$60 < a \leqslant 80$	4.15
$80 < a \leqslant 90$	1

(Class widths used to calculate the frequency density)

4 (a)

Weight, *w* (kg)	Frequency
$30 < w \leqslant 40$	34
$40 < w \leqslant 50$	62
$50 < w \leqslant 55$	22
$55 < w \leqslant 60$	19
$60 < w \leqslant 85$	30

(b) Total number of sharks = 167

5 (a)

Waiting time, *t* (min)	Frequency
$0 \leqslant t < 10$	32
$10 \leqslant t < 15$	20
$15 \leqslant t < 30$	18
$30 \leqslant t < 35$	5
$35 \leqslant t$	0

(b)

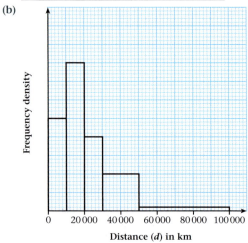

6 (a)

Distance, *d* (km)	Frequency
$0 \leqslant d < 10\,000$	25
$10\,000 \leqslant d < 20\,000$	40
$20\,000 \leqslant d < 30\,000$	20
$30\,000 \leqslant d < 50\,000$	20
$50\,000 \leqslant d < 100\,000$	5

(b)

Mixed exercise 2

1

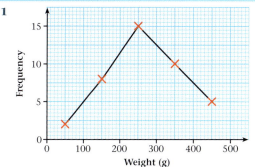

2

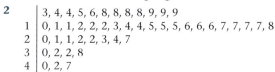

```
  | 3, 4, 4, 5, 6, 8, 8, 8, 8, 9, 9, 9
1 | 0, 1, 1, 2, 2, 2, 3, 4, 4, 5, 5, 5, 6, 6, 6, 7, 7, 7, 7, 8
2 | 0, 1, 1, 2, 2, 3, 4, 7
3 | 0, 2, 2, 8
4 | 0, 2, 7
5 | 1, 2, 7          Key: 5|1 means 51
```

3 The modal price range for Make 1 is £15 000–£20 000, compared to £5000–£10 000 for Make 2.

Make 1

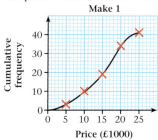

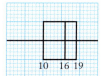

Make 2

The median price of Make 1 is £8000 greater than the median price of Make 2.
The lower quartile price of Make 1 is £4000 greater than the lower quartile of Make 2.
The upper quartile price of Make 1 is £7000 greater than the upper quartile price of Make 2.
The interquartile range of prices of Make 1 is £3000 greater than the interquartile range of price of Make 2.
We can say Make 1 cars are more expensive than Make 2.

4 (a)

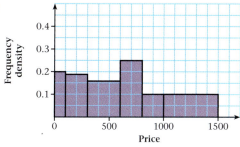

(b)

Price, p (in £)	Frequency
$0 < p \leq 100$	20
$100 < p \leq 300$	36
$300 < p \leq 600$	48
$600 < p \leq 800$	50
$800 < p \leq 1000$	20
$1000 < p \leq 1500$	50

5 (a)

Time, t (min)	Frequency
$20 < t \leq 25$	20
$25 < t \leq 40$	42
$40 < t \leq 60$	48
$60 < t \leq 85$	30
$85 < t \leq 90$	6

(b) There are 146 students.

6 (a)

Height, h (1000 m)	Frequency Olympus	Frequency Newton
$0 \leq h < 2$	0	0
$2 \leq h < 4$	1	2
$4 \leq h < 6$	1	4
$6 \leq h < 8$	3	7
$8 \leq h < 10$	4	2
$10 \leq h < 12$	2	1
$12 \leq h < 14$	0	0

(b)

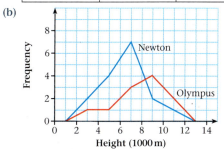

(c) Generally the mountains are higher in the Olympus region. The distribution is further to the right.

7

Number of emails, x	Frequency
$0 < x \leq 5$	40
$5 < x \leq 10$	20
$10 < x \leq 25$	75
$25 < x \leq 35$	30
$35 < x \leq 60$	50

8 (a)

Mass, m (g)	Frequency
$0 < m \leqslant 100$	7
$100 < m \leqslant 150$	26
$150 < m \leqslant 200$	30
$200 < m \leqslant 250$	35
$250 < m \leqslant 400$	12

(b)

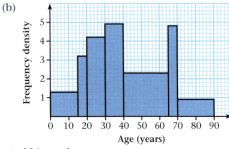

(c) 110   **(d)** 0.43 (2 d.p.)

9 (a)

Age, a (years)	Frequency
$0 < a \leqslant 15$	20
$15 < a \leqslant 20$	16
$20 < a \leqslant 30$	42
$30 < a \leqslant 40$	49
$40 < a \leqslant 65$	57
$65 < a \leqslant 70$	24
$70 < a \leqslant 90$	18

(b)

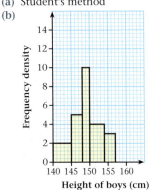

(c) 226 people

(d) 70 people; assuming that the 20–30 interval is split evenly, i.e., 21 people are aged between 20 and 25, and 21 people are aged between 25 and 30.

10 (a) Student's method

(b)

Height of boys (cm)

(c)

Heights of girls, h (cm)	Frequency
$140 \leqslant h < 146$	6
$146 \leqslant h < 150$	8
$150 \leqslant h < 151$	12
$151 \leqslant h < 152$	13
$152 \leqslant h < 155$	21
$155 < h < 160$	10

(d) The range of the boys' heights is less than the range of the girls' heights.
The modal class interval for the boys' height (148–150 cm) is less than the modal class interval for the girls' height (151–152 cm).

11

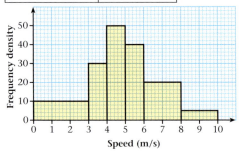

12

Speed, s (m/s)	Frequency
$0 < s \leqslant 3$	30
$3 < s \leqslant 4$	30
$4 < s \leqslant 5$	50
$5 < s \leqslant 6$	40
$6 < s \leqslant 8$	40
$8 < s \leqslant 10$	10

13 (a) $x = 15$

(b) Disagree. Since 31 lies within a class interval it is impossible to say exactly how many candidates got 31 or more.
We can estimate, by assuming the 30–35 class is evenly spread so that the number of candidates getting 31 or more and less than 35 is 80, but this gives an estimate of $80 + 140 + 50 = 270$ which is more than half the number of candidates.

Exercise 3A

1 (a) 2 goals   **(b)** 1 goal   **(c)** 1.35 goals
2 (a) 2   **(b)** 28 cm²
3 (a) 42   **(b)** 33   **(c)** 13
4 (a) 4 days   **(b)** 1 day
5 6.5
6 (a) 1 certificate   **(b)** 1.7 certificates
    (c) 2 certificates
7 (a) 4 people   **(b)** 4.01 people   **(c)** 6 people

Exercise 3B

1 (a) 35–40 minutes
   (b) 34.75 minutes or 34 min 45 secs
2 (a) 38.4 mph (3 s.f.)
   (b) $40 < s \leq 50$ mph
   (c) $30 < s \leq 40$ mph
   (d) 21 cars
   (e) As we do not know the spread of the speeds of the vehicles in the second survey, we cannot say whether the conclusion is correct or not.
3 (a) $20 < d \leq 30$
   (b) $20 < d \leq 30$
   (c) 28.4 light years (3 s.f.)
   (d) 95 light years
   (e) As we do not know the spread of the distances in the second constellation we cannot make a sound comparison. The mean may be affected by a few very short distances.

Exercise 3C

1 (a)

Number of throws	Cumulative frequency
1 to 5	10
1 to 10	27
1 to 15	38
1 to 20	43
1 to 25	55
1 to 30	75

(b)

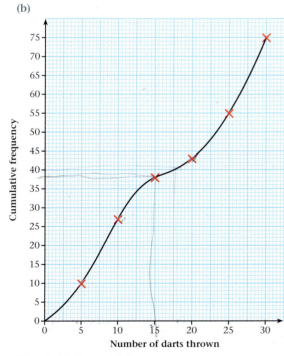

Number of darts thrown

(c) (i) Median = 15 darts
   (ii) Upper quartile = 25 darts,
       lower quartile = 8 darts
   (iii) Interquartile range = 17 darts
   (iv) 25%

(d)

2 (a)

Waiting time in seconds	Cumulative frequency
Up to 60	4
Up to 120	12
Up to 180	22
Up to 240	40
Up to 300	70
Up to 360	80

(b)

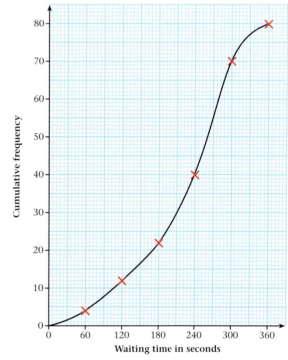

Waiting time in seconds

(c) (i) Median = 240 seconds
   (ii) Interquartile range = 108 seconds

(d)

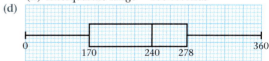

Exercise 3D

1 (a)

Weekly rainfall (mm)	Cumulative frequency
Up to 10	18
Up to 20	38
Up to 30	44
Up to 40	47
Up to 50	50
Up to 60	52

(b)

Cumulative frequency graph with Weekly rainfall in mm on the x-axis (0 to 60) and Cumulative frequency on the y-axis (0 to 55).

(c) Median = 12 mm
(d) Interquartile range = 12 mm
(e) 20 weeks
(f)

Box plots for Gatwick and Manchester on a scale from 0 to 40.

The box plots for Gatwick and Manchester airports show that the median weekly rainfall at Manchester is greater than the median weekly rainfall at Gatwick. In fact, the median weekly rainfall at Manchester is just more than the upper quartile weekly rainfall at Gatwick, so there is a very significant number of weeks at Manchester with weekly rainfall greater than the upper quartile weekly rainfall at Gatwick. We can say with confidence that the weekly rainfall in Manchester is generally greater than at Gatwick. Any comment about the lower quartiles is inconclusive.

2 (a) The interquartile range for boys is larger than that for girls. The median weight for boys is higher than the median weight for girls; in fact, the median weight for boys is higher than the upper quartile weight for girls, so there is a very significant number of boys with weights greater than the upper quartile weight for girls. The lower quartile weight for boys is higher than the median weight for girls, so there can be relatively few boys with a weight less than the median weight for girls. We can say with confidence that the boys in the sample are generally heavier than the girls.

(b)

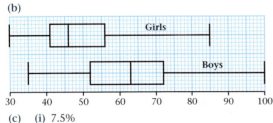

Box plots for Girls and Boys on a scale from 30 to 100.

(c) (i) 7.5%
     (ii) 47.5%

3 The possible marks were the same for both exams, but the median, lower quartile and upper quartile were all higher for the geography exam, so it is likely that was easier than the science exam.

Mixed exercise 3

1 (a)

Time, t (hours)	Cumulative frequency
$50 \leqslant t < 55$	12
$50 \leqslant t < 60$	33
$50 \leqslant t < 65$	69
$50 \leqslant t < 70$	92
$50 \leqslant t < 75$	100

(b)

Cumulative frequency graph with Time (hours) on the x-axis (0 to 70) and Cumulative frequency on the y-axis (0 to 100).

(c) 62 hours

2 The median height in Village B is 6 cm greater than the median height in Village A.
The lower quartile height of Village B is 4 cm greater than the lower quartile height of Village A.
The upper quartile height of Village B is 5 cm greater than the upper quartile height of Village A.
The interquartile range of heights of Village B is 1 cm greater than the interquartile range of heights of Village A.
It is fair to say that the people in Village B are taller than those in Village A.

3 No, it is not fair. We have only an average to compare and not also a range. It is possible that, for example, 75% of people at Spencer and Sons are paid more than the maximum amount paid to people at Creswell Ltd.

4 The median average house price in 2001 is £50 000 greater than the median average house price in 1991.
The lower quartile average house price in 2001 is £35 000 greater than the lower quartile average house price in 1991.
The upper quartile average house price in 2001 is £60 000 greater than the upper quartile average house price in 1991.
The interquartile range of average house prices in 2001 is £25 000 greater than the interquartile range of average house prices in 1991.
We can say that the average house prices in 2001 are greater than the average house prices in 1991.

5 (a) 26–30
(b) 11–15
(c) Estimate for mean number of marks is 16.3

6

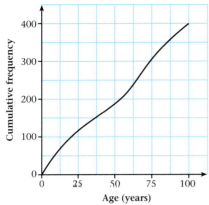

7 (a) $200 < l \leq 300$ ppm

(b)

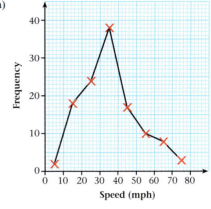

(c) 258.75 ppm

(d)

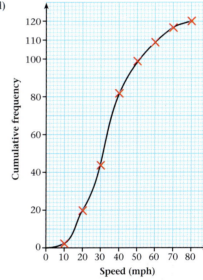

(e) (i) 260 ppm
(ii) 110 ppm

(f)

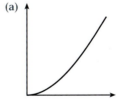

8 (a)

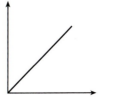

(b) 30 mph–40 mph
(c) 35.6 mph (1 d.p.)
(d)

(e) (i) 34 mph
(ii) 19 mph
(iii) 16 vehicles
(f)

9 (a)   (b)

(c)

10 (a) 473 mph

(b)
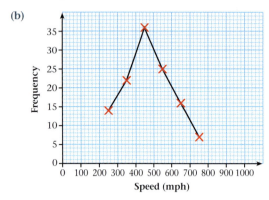

(c)

Speed	Cumulative frequency
Up to 300 mph	14
Up to 400 mph	36
Up to 500 mph	72
Up to 600 mph	97
Up to 700 mph	113
Up to 800 mph	120

(d)
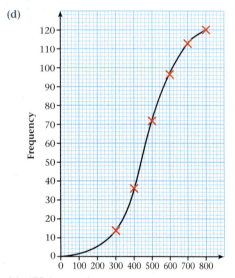

(e) 470 (approx.)

(f) **(i)** 380
   (ii) 570
   (iii) 190

(g)
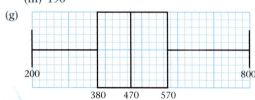

11
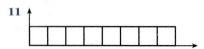

12 PC, QD, RB, SA

Exercise 4A

1 (a), (b)
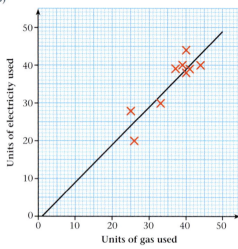

(c) The scatter diagram shows positive correlation.
(d) The estimate is 35 units of electricity used.

2 (a) The scatter diagram shows positive correlation.
(b)
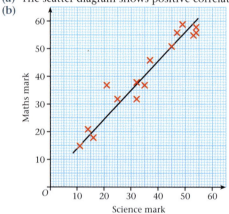

(c) 48 marks

3 (a) There is positive correlation between X and Y.
(b)
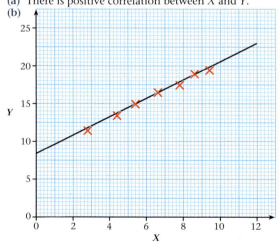

(c) $Y = 1.4X + 7$

Exercise 4B

1 (a)

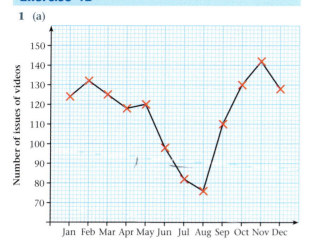

(b) Moving averages:

1st	2nd	3rd	4th	5th	6th
124.75	123.75	115.25	104.5	94	91.5

7th	8th	9th
99.5	114.5	127.5

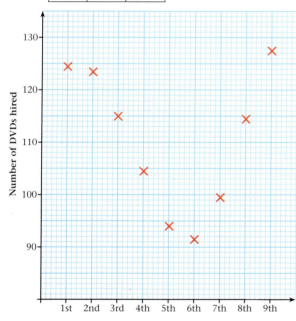

(c) The number of issues of videos falls during the first half of the year and then rises at the end of the year.

2 (a)

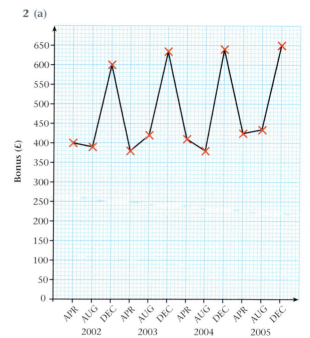

(b) (c) Moving averages:

1st	2nd	3rd	4th	5th	6th
$463\frac{1}{3}$	$456\frac{2}{3}$	$466\frac{2}{3}$	$478\frac{1}{3}$	$488\frac{1}{3}$	475

7th	8th	9th	10th
$476\frac{2}{3}$	$481\frac{2}{3}$	500	$503\frac{1}{3}$

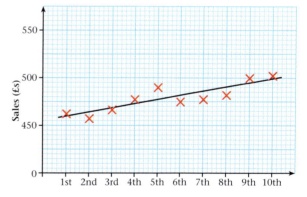

y intercept, $c = 450$
Gradient, $m = \frac{30}{9} = 3.\dot{3}$
Equation $S = 3.3x + 450$
where S is the quantity of sales and x is the number of 4-month periods after Dec 2001.

(e) The graphs show there is a slight increase in Jon's bonus over the period from April 2002 to December 2005.

3 (a) Moving averages

1st	2nd	3rd
288	297.75	300.5

(b) The moving averages show an increasing trend.

Exercise 4C

1 £15 725.02

2 76p

3 Assuming bread prices follow the changes in the RPI, a similar loaf would cost 4p.

4 (a)

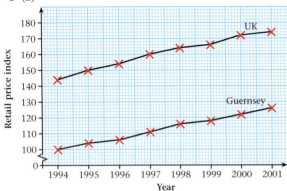

(b) (c)

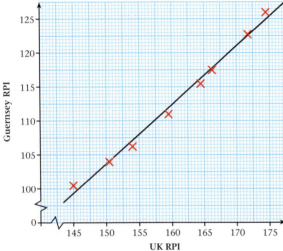

(d) Scatter graph shows positive correlation between the UK and Guernsey RPIs

(e) Proportional changes to RPI have been:

UK: $\frac{174.6}{145.0} = 1.204$ Guernsey: $\frac{125.9}{100.2} = 1.256$

Increase in RPI is less for UK than for Guernsey. So, no evidence to support claim.

Mixed exercise 4

1 (a) 48.1 million

(b)

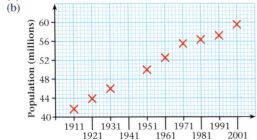

(c) The population shows an increasing trend.

2 (a) and (c)

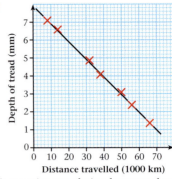

(b) There is negative correlation between depth of tread and distance travelled.

(d) About 70 000 km

3 (a) (i) 18.5 cm   (ii) 41 cm

(b) (i) is more likely to be reliable as we have no data about height after 16 days

(c) $y = 1.6x + 1$

4 (a) (c)

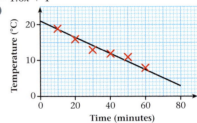

(b) The graph shows negative correlation.

(d) About 93 minutes

(e) $y = 21 - 0.23x$

5 (a) and (b)

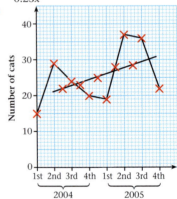

(c) There is an increasing trend in the number of cats born.

6 (a) and (b)

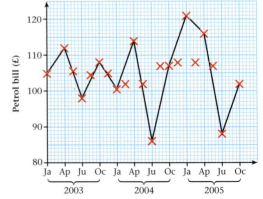

(c) The 4-point moving average stayed in the £100–£110 band, but show a slight upward trend over time.

7 (a) and (b)

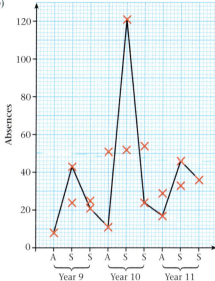

(c) Each year absences are highest in the spring. The 3-point moving averages are affected by the abnormally high Year 10 Spring absences which mask a generally upward trend from Year 9 to Year 11.

8 28p   9 £30.81

Exercise 5A

1 (a) $\frac{1}{5}$ (b) $\frac{3}{5}$ (c) $\frac{13}{20}$ (d) $\frac{3}{10}$
2 Take a sample of trains by doing a survey, and count how many trains are late. The number of trains that are late divided by the total number of trains in the survey is an estimate for the probability of a train being late. The larger the sample, the more accurate the estimate.
3 (a) (i) Estimate for the probability of match finishing with exactly 4 goals scored is 0.11, since from the results in the surve y the number of matches ending with 4 goals scored was 22 out of 200.
     (ii) Estimate for the probability of match finishing with 4 or more goals scored is 0.19, since from the results in the survey the number of matches ending with 4 or more goals scored was 38 out of 200.
   (b) 2496 games
4 Estimate for the likely number of times spinner will land on B is 108
5 (a) Spinning the spinner is an event governed by the laws of chance and so the outcomes are determined by laws of probability. It is likely that repeating the same experiment will not give the same results so we will get a different set of outcomes.
   (b) A 0.315, B 0.275, C 0.195, D 0.215
   (c) The spinner appears to be biased. The theoretical probability of landing on each letter is 0.25.

Exercise 5B

1 London by car   Bristol by car
  London by bus   Bristol by bus
  London by train   Bristol by train
  Manchester by car   Edinburgh by car
  Manchester by bus   Edinburgh by bus
  Manchester by train   Edinburgh by train

2 (a) (A, 1); (A, 2); (A, 3); (A, 4); (A, 5); (A, 6)
      (B, 1); (B, 2); (B, 3); (B, 4); (B, 5); (B, 6)
      (C, 1); (C, 2); (C, 3); (C, 4); (C, 5); (C, 6)
   (b) $\frac{1}{18}$ (c) 0
3 (a) (R, 1); (R, 2); (R, 3)   (B, 1); (B, 2); (B, 3)
      (W, 1); (W, 2); (W, 3)
   (b) $\frac{1}{9}$
4 (a) (H, 1); (H, 2); (H, 3); (H, 4); (H, 5); (H, 6)
      (T, 1); (T, 2); (T, 3); (T, 4); (T, 5); (T, 6)
   (b) $\frac{1}{12}$

Exercise 5C

1 (a) 0.23   (b) 166
2 (a) 0.63   (b) 0.07   (c) 0.97
3 (a) 0.48   (b) 0.92
4 (a) 0.15
   (b) (i) 0.0324   (ii) 0.1704   (iii) 0.0547
5 (a) $\frac{1}{32}$ (b) $\frac{31}{32}$
6 (a)

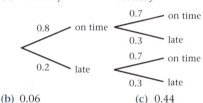

   (b) 0.06   (c) 0.44

Mixed exercis 5

1 (a) Spinning the spinner is an event governed by the laws of chance and so the outcomes are determined by laws of probability. It is likely that repeating the same experiment will not give the same results so we will get a different set of outcomes.
   (b) (i) $\frac{37}{150}$ (ii) $\frac{1}{10}$ (iii) $\frac{8}{25}$
2 Estimate for the likely number of times spinner will stop on C is 204.
3 If the spinner was not biased we would have P(A) = P(B) = P(C) = P(D) = P(E) = 0.2 i.e. we would expect each letter to come up about 2000 times. In fact, B came up 4009 times, A 593 times and C 1427 times, which suggests the spinner is biased in favour of B. It appears to be biased against A and, to a lesser degree, C.
4 (a) 0.225   (b) 0.475   (c) 0.525
5 (a) Morning   Afternoon

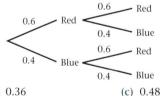

   (b) 0.36   (c) 0.48
6 0.52
7 465
8 (a) Tennis   Snooker

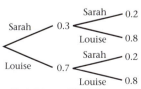

   (b) (i) 0.06   (ii) 0.94   (c) 24 times

9 (a) 0.97   (b) 18 000 batteries
    (c) 0.000 027; the events: '1st battery faulty', '2nd battery faulty', 3rd battery faulty' are independent, so P(all 3 batteries faulty) = P(1st faulty) × (2nd faulty) × P(3rd faulty) = 0.03 × 0.03 × 0.03

10 (a) 0.9997   (b) 3600

11 (a) 0.14   (b) 0.76

12 (a)

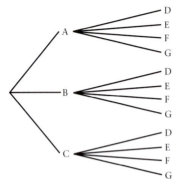

    (b) A & D, A & E, A & F, A & G, B & D, B & E, B & F, B & G, C & D, C & E, C & F, C & G

Exercise 6A

1 (a) $\frac{7}{15}$ (b) $\frac{7}{15}$

2 (a)

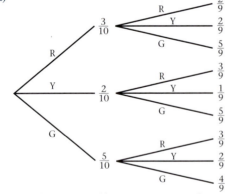

    (b) (i) $\frac{1}{7}$ (ii) $\frac{17}{35}$ (iii) $\frac{18}{35}$

3 $\frac{14}{285}$ **4** $\frac{47}{120}$ **5** $\frac{47}{120}$

Mixed exercise 6

1 (a)

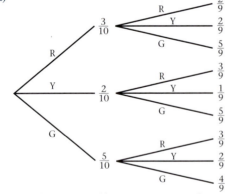

    (b) (i) $\frac{1}{15}$ (ii) $\frac{14}{45}$ (iii) $\frac{7}{15}$

2 (a) $\frac{1}{6}$ (b) $\frac{5}{36}$ (c) $\frac{5^4}{6^5} = \frac{625}{7776}$

3 (a) $\frac{39}{56}$ (b) $\frac{17}{56}$

4 $\frac{1}{26}$

5 (a) $\frac{37}{60}$ (b) $\frac{23}{60}$

6 (a) $\frac{1}{120}$ (b) $\frac{7}{40}$

7 0.645

8 (a) (i) $\frac{3}{25}$ (ii) $\frac{2}{5}$
    (b) $\frac{33}{115}$

Examination practice paper: Higher

Section A

1 (a) 0.55   (b) 0.45

2 $\frac{63}{30} = 2.1$

3

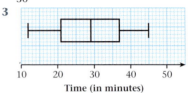

4 (a) 8, 12
    (b)

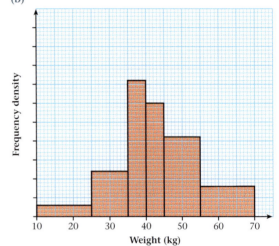

Section B

1 (a) (c)

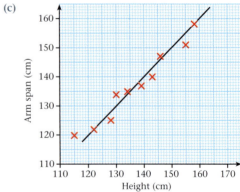

    (b) Positive correlation   (d) about 150 cm

2 The question needs a period of time, e.g. 'at the weekend'; it needs to say 'to the nearest hour' or the times on the answer boxes should be given as a range; more answer boxes may be required.

3 (a) $15 \leqslant t < 20$ (b) 10.75 hours (c) 8

4 $\frac{42}{90}$ or $\frac{7}{15}$